# GROUNDED

## WHAT YOU SHOULD KNOW
## ABOUT OWNING A CAFÉ

**BEN COYLE & PETAR JURCIC**

# ACKNOWLEDGEMENTS

*Petar:*

To my amazing parents – I am who I am because of you. Thank you is never enough. Hvala vam i volim vas puno!

To my beautiful wife Vanessa – Every crazy dream and ambition gets your support. Thank you for loving me unconditionally and allowing me to follow my journey, and for always encouraging me to do what makes me happy. I love you.

To my baby girl Lucinda – I could never put into words how much love I have for you. You're my everything. It's all for you. The future is yours to create...dream big, and know I'll always be there. Voli te Tata xx.

To Ben - Thanks for letting me hitch my wagon to your experience! This collaboration has been brilliant as we've shared knowledge, banter - and of course many coffees. It's just the beginning….

*Ben:*

To my mother Gaye Reeves, who has always kept me grounded, to who I owe everything and who was always there with support, wisdom and love......and soup. Love always.

To all my customers and staff, thank you for all the lessons, whether a good or bad experience at the time it was always part of the journey. Always more smiles than tears. Thank you.

To Petar, in the short time since we met I have loved your enthusiasm, work ethic and passion for helping people and it has been a pleasure to work on this with you. I look forward to helping the dreams of many come true in the future as we share our experiences and knowledge with others around the world.

Special thanks from us both to Ronan Leonard for being the middle man for our introduction. The power of networking!

# COPYRIGHT

First published in 2018 by "The Café Guys"

National Library of Australia Cataloguing-in-Publication entry

Creators: Petar Jurcic and Ben Coyle

Title: Grounded; What you should know about owning a cafe

ISBN: 9780994354075

### Disclaimer

# CONTENTS

# INTRODUCTIONS

### Ben on Petar

*I met Petar in late 2017 via an introduction from a mutual business associate. I was greatly impressed by Petar's passion for business and coaching others. He was a successful Human Resources professional who was looking for fulfilment in other areas of his life. He was passionate about fitness, wellbeing, nutrition and people and saw that owning and operating a cafe would fill some of this need. He successfully owned, operated and sold his cafe around the time he and his wife were expecting their first child. He now coaches other people in all facets of life. One thing that struck me was his intense want to help others and make others journeys easier particularly in the hospitality industry - something that we both share. Petar brings solid business and corporate experience into the fold and successfully balances having a young family, his health and fitness and his business life. For more information on Petar go to www.the5argroup.com.*

### Petar on Ben

*At a networking group, a mutual associate told me about Ben and his cafe, and offered to make the introduction as he felt there was much in common with our respective paths. Like myself, Ben opened a hospitality business with very little experience coming from a background as a Customs Dog Handler. He was looking to create a space that would connect others and be a staple in the community. 15 years later, its safe to say he's done just that. However, there is so much more. Ben's commitment and purpose to help others through his wealth of experience, both in Australia and abroad, is outstanding. Business minded, focused and easygoing, it was very easy to work with Ben on this project, with a view to help others who are thinking about running or already own a cafe or restaurant. To learn more about Ben, visit www.thecafeguy.com.au/.*

We were going to open the introduction with some hard hitting facts about how many businesses fail in the first five years however we thought better of it. Neither do we wish to be fluffy and tell you it's all roses.

Opening a café business may be one of the most challenging and rewarding experiences you'll ever have. 'Yeah right', I hear you say, 'Everyone is just going to love my café as I will have the best coffee, the best food and I am going to take baths in all my cash'. Well that is my wish for you. Unfortunately for a large percentage, you'll be struggling to find 50 cents to plug the bathtub. If you are serious about setting off on this remarkable journey and want a bit of advice, buy this book if you haven't already. It will pay itself off over your journey, most likely over and over again…otherwise we sincerely wish you luck. As with any challenging journey, you will hit bumps in the road, encounter difficult customers and you will make mistakes. In fact, any successful entrepreneur, business person or corporate CEO will admit that making mistakes is crucial to their growth. Thomas Edison took 10,000 attempts to invent the light globe. Whether it's a staff issue, a financial issue or how you deal with a customer, the key is to reduce the impact of those mistakes on you, your business and those around you. We have made many mistakes over the years in business, and have tried to mention as many of them as possible in this book. However, through perseverance, flexibility, openness to change and trying new ideas, hard work and the occasional stroke of genius, our businesses have thrived. We've learnt that mistakes are blessings in disguise and, if you can keep a mindset of being thankful for them, you'll have learned a valuable lesson and be unlikely to repeat them. In this book, our aim is to share our experiences so that you can learn from them and achieve the same success in your own hospitality business while (hopefully) avoiding the same mistakes.

### Petar's Story
After completing a Bachelor of Business and spending the better part of a decade working in Human Resource Management, I began to feel unfulfilled. I was lacking passion, motivation and was disillusioned with my career path. I felt lost. How could this be? I was in a secure and well-paying job with holiday and sick pay. I had everything I was lead to believe I wanted. I was masking my pain from others, while inside I knew I was on a road to depression.

2

This is where I learnt an important lesson. My values weren't congruent with how I was living my life, and the only thing that could bring me closer to feeling at peace was to make a choice. I made a decision and took action to change my circumstances.

I considered what my passions were – the things that lit me up, the things I enjoyed and could create a potential living from. The 3 big themes were health and fitness, people, and business. I didn't want to go back to school or undertake more formal education. I wanted to get out there and just do it.

After some research and planning, I felt like I could combine these passions into a health-based café business. Despite the café and restaurant industry in Melbourne is one of the most ruthless, and despite having no experience in cafes or running a business, I was determined and confident I could succeed. I quit my job and changed the trajectory of my life forever.

As a result of going in with eyes wide open, applying discipline, focus and a relentless work ethic – I did it. I created and ran a successful and profitable business against all odds and advice. It fast became one of the most popular cafes in Melbourne's West. The sense of satisfaction and fulfilment is indescribable.

However, it wasn't just about the profits. It was even more. It was about what I learnt in the process, who I became and the people I attracted and built relationships with. I was working countless more hours for considerably less pay than in my corporate career, but I felt like I was finally in tune. I closed the gap between who I was being and who I needed to be. This is something I am now passionate about sharing with and creating for my clients.

Through my experience, I have now made it my mission to help others achieve success on their terms through my consulting business The 5AR Group and as one half of "The Cafe Guys". My goal now is to be the person I would have wanted in my life when I was feeling lost and needing direction, structure and clarity.

### Ben's Story
Many of us feel we're destined to do more, or crave to do more, than an ordinary, day-to-day, nine-to-five job. Even with flexible hours, the drudgery of heading

into work is so numbing that sometimes we dream about doing our own thing, enjoying the romanticism of being our own boss and master of our destiny. I was one of those dreamers, and my fulfilment came in the form of a café. However, unlike a lot of people, I never dreamed of owning a café – becoming a café owner was serendipitous. It came about as a result of something else I was interested in. I was a detector dog handler for the Australian Customs Service as it was known in those days, a job that many people found interesting, but something in me searched for more. In my time as a handler, I dabbled in a few small businesses. I tried my hand as a part-time fitness/aerobics instructor and a masseur. I did some courses in basic Chinese medicine and natural healing. A lot of my friends looked at me sideways, especially when I was dabbling in the healing arts, and I must admit that marrying a government job with what many thought of as tree-hugging pursuits was a bit strange. I always had an entrepreneurial streak. I set out to start a healing venue that offered all the things I wanted to try – such as yoga, African drumming, belly dance, Tai Chi – as well as being a place to get a massage or even a clairvoyant reading. While a café was part of the venture, it was only meant to be a coffee and cake arrangement that supported the spiritual activities.

I started my venture because I wanted to help people, but my naivety almost brought me down within the first two years. I didn't understand business. You can be as spiritual as you like, but you cannot ignore the rules of business... which in itself is a journey of personal growth. I started the Dancing Dog Café as a sole trader (I'm tempted to write soul trader), and it transitioned from a healing venue to a café with a strong spiritual undertone, one that accommodated classes as well as an art gallery, live music and poetry readings. It even had live theatre at one point. This business eventually became a partnership and a more bar-focused venue, but one that still exudes a community spirit some fifteen years later. It also continues to support the performing arts, including live music, comedy, poetry and the odd theatre show. Dancing Dog Café has been reinvented several times and the only constant of the business is change. I've realised that it still achieves my original goal of providing healing, but now it does that by being a warm, welcoming and safe venue where people meet and make friends.

# How to use this book

We hope this book will be helpful to those of you who are starting out on the journey into the world of business and, in particular, are looking at the hospitality industry. The four parts will give you an overview of what you need to consider when turning your idea into a successful hospitality business, including building the foundations you need to grow, how to attract loyal customers, diversifying and empire building, and your final exit.

We hope some of the stories are amusing and make you laugh. We also hope when the going does get tough, that you feel you aren't alone. Regardless you can't ever fail in business, whatever the outcome is. You will always grow and learn from your experiences and can use the knowledge in future dealings. Our aim is to help you get over the line and assist you in creating a viable business that defies the statistics.

We have filled this book with tips that can save you money and make you money, and a few ideas to assist in getting your business moving quicker. You'll find suggestions to follow, important things to consider and information that may save you anything from the price of this book to hundreds, if not thousands of dollars over the life of your business.

Throughout the book, you will find referrals to our website (www.thecafeguys.com.au) where you can obtain further information. There you will find tools that can help you create your business plan and start turning your dream of owning a café into reality.

Ultimately, the journey is yours and every road is different, but if you follow just one tip it might pay for this book multiple times over.

With that said, enjoy the journey and share with us how you're going!

**Petar and Ben**

THE CAFE GUYS

# PART 1
# IN THE BEGINNING

# CHAPTER 1

# MAKING THE DECISION

T here are several things you need to consider before stepping out into the business world, including your level of commitment, the financial cost of starting up and the potential reactions of friends and family. These are all part of the process of making the decision.

Why am I doing this?

Before you answer the following questions it's important to take time and consider exactly that. Many people believe it is a way to achieve a certain lifestyle, to fulfil a dream or just love the idea of owning or running their own place. Your reason is your reason and that is absolutely ok, just be clear as you go through this book about why you are doing what you are doing.

Are you 100% committed? Businesses change over or close down at a high rate so you have to ask yourself "Am I committed enough to put in the hard work, the long hours and, (for some) deal with a lot of pressure and stress?"

As you read through keep revisiting your answers and make sure that you are going into business with your eyes wide open.

• Why are you considering starting a café?
• What is your vision?
• How may this improve your life (pros)?
• How may it negatively impact your life (cons)?

Make notes and keep track of your plans and ideas. With the aim of you starting off on the right foot and a certain level of realism, it is important that you think of both the positives and negatives.

**Petar:**

*I attribute the success of my cafe to creating a solid foundation before I served my first coffee or even had a place to operate out of. That was in the form of being clear to myself as to why I was doing this, and what it was going to give me from a personal fulfilment point of view. Just as important was the "eyes wide open" part. As fun as it is in the planning, design and preparation stage if you aren't prepared to put in the hard work and long hours when it's needed – especially the unglamorous jobs – then this industry may not be for you. However, if you have the determination and work ethic to step up whenever is required and do whatever needs to be done, then you're giving yourself the best possible chance at success already.*

### How much will it cost?

How much do you need to start up? The answer will depend on a number of factors.

How much you need will depend on whether you buy an existing business or start from an empty space; your style; design and taste… all of which are discussed further on.

Lack of capital is a major reason business don't survive. You need to be able to finance not just the start of your business, but also possible quieter periods in the early stages of your business that will affect your income.

This is especially important if you have dependents.

Even though this will be discussed in some more detail, the cost will be influenced by what you envision. The style and design will influence how much you'll need to spend on furniture and fittings whereas the type of food you plan to serve will influence the equipment you'll need for your kitchen.

**Ben:**

*I started my café with $25,000 and personal credit (not recommended), I had reserve funds and used a bit of superannuation. I figure with reinvestment it cost me slightly over $100,000.*

**Petar:**

*Taking over a previously closed café which was already furnished in a style consistent with my theme and vision, all I needed was some minor and relatively cheap cosmetic changes which cost around $5,000 all up, and I was ready to open. Over time we reinvested, but I was always mindful to do it in a cost-effective manner.*

### Will I survive?

We both left well-paid and secure jobs to start up our respective cafés with little to no experience. We encourage you to do some basic finance to understand what your business needs to make in order to provide a viable replacement income.

There are no rules on when, and sometimes unfortunately if, you will turn a profit. There is no guarantee at all, however, most Australian small businesses expect a return within three years. The following is a very simple guide and dependent on how well you operate your business.

To give you an idea of what you need your business to earn to replace your current income, consider how much you're currently earning (inclusive of any benefits). This is the amount you'll need to make in profit – not just takings – to replace your income and maintain your current lifestyle.

Based on the Australian model, you would take that figure and multiply it by three. For example, if you currently earn $100,000 per annum you'll need to turn over at least $300,000 per annum.

This is working on the basic equation of one-third expenses, one-third staff and one-third profit (which you'll have to pay tax on).

Create a formula for yourself:
- Set your target income e.g. $100,000

- Add your anticipated overheads (rent, electricity, stock, wages, etc.) e.g. + $200,000

- Divide it by the number of days you expect to be open (factor in Public Holidays, and how many days per week you will operate). E.g. $300,000 / 300 days (6 days per week, 2 weeks off) = $1,000 per day average required to achieve target income.

- Divide by expected average customer spend. E.g. $1,000 / $4 = 250 customers per day required spending an average $4 to achieve your annual target income.

It's a basic exercise and obviously not exactly as you may charge less or more, or be open less or more days, however, you need to think about a rough average sale per customer so you can pay your bills and make money. Adjust your own variables as necessary and see what you come up with and what to aim for. Remember, while it's all about the journey, the goal is to profit in order to fulfil why you're doing this, as discussed earlier.

*Ben:*

*Whether this is a passion, a dream, a retirement plan or something else, in a business you need to make a profit.*

*This may sound like an obvious statement, but it isn't and wasn't for me when I first started in business. I was always trying to help others first until I realised that I couldn't give what I didn't have. I had a problem with accepting money, which remained a self-defeating attitude for some time. While money isn't everything, it is important and must be accepted in every way. It is a fair exchange for the service you provide.*

## What will people say?

If the figures are right, you'll probably reach a point when you decide to go ahead with your plans. It is likely that you will have to deal with the fears and opinions of family, friends and others.

If you're lucky, you might know people who have business experience to draw on and can give you honest and unbiased opinions. If not, simply listen to opinions and advice, but remember that the decision is ultimately yours. Look at what others say as objectively as possible. Use any negativity or pessimism to your advantage, not necessarily to prove others wrong, but rather to prove yourself right.

Speak with experienced business owners and advisors. Café owners are ideal, but ultimately the type of business doesn't matter as similarities exist across most businesses, especially small business. A lot of issues that small business owners experience are not isolated to that specific business. Don't feel that a café owner is the only person who has good advice for you. We all have marketing, advertising, staffing, buying and selling, design and web related issues and experience.

Listen to the advice you are given but trust your instincts. Many fears you face may not be your own but those of people with good intentions, but uninformed advice, and most of the time it will come from those close to you. Take everything in and base your decision on how you feel deep within.

## Putting it all together

To decide whether opening a café is the right decision for you, you need to consider all of these variables. Here is a mini checklist that we suggest you use before making the decision to go forward. You need to be able to confidently tick off each item before you start:

• I have made a decision to go ahead and I am 100 per cent committed.

- I have an idea of how much finance I will need.
- I have worked out the income I need to sustain my standard of living.
- I have discussed my decision with family and/or friends.
- Whatever the outcome, I'm prepared to learn from my mistakes in order to achieve.

# CHAPTER 2

# FIRST STEPS

So, you've made your decision – you're going to do it. What next? We both started with next to no business experience and had never seriously worked in hospitality other than helping out some friends or short-lived fast-food jobs in our teens. If we can do it, so can you. Starting a business can be a bit like building a house; it feels chaotic with lots of things happening at the same time. But in the beginning there was a plan, so let's start with that.

### What's in a name?

If you don't already have a name for your café it is worth starting to write down names that resonate with you. You are going to have to register a business name at some point.

You will need to go to a business database website, (www.asic.gov.au in Australia) where you can search if names have been taken and search that the domain name on the web is available.

### Petar:

*For some reason, the word "Crimson" came up early on and any other words I was considering were in association with "Crimson". I liked the word itself and also the shade of red that we could then use throughout our branding and theme. I settled on "Crimson Bear" because it was catchy, made a very easy logo and brand, and the bear is a reference to the animal native to the mountains and forests where my parents are from in Croatia.*

### Ben:

*I wrote out a variety of names and whittled away at them until I came back to the first one. Some names are memorable, some are cool, some aren't. Just pick something that you like and can relate to. The Dancing Dog Café worked for me because I used to work with dogs, I was born in the year of the dog (Chinese astrology), lots of people love dogs and the area is home to the Western Bulldogs, the local football team. People still called it other names like*

*"The Dirty Dog" or "The Barking Dog", but always remember the "Dog" which is what it is affectionately nicknamed by patrons.*

## Visualisation

### Ben:

*I love the scene from Willy Wonka and the Chocolate Factory (1971) where Gene Wilder pauses on the steps of his garden and says 'We are the dreamers of dreams'. This is your dream, so take a moment to create it in your mind.*

Visualisation is a concept that appears in many self-development and business books. Before you begin your business planning, take ten minutes to close your eyes and visualise your café. Imagine the colours and decor. Imagine walking in the door and seeing your staff greeting you. Watch them taking orders. Focus on what the business looks and feels like. What do you want people to feel when they come in? Chic and trendy, warm like a hug, stepping back in time or super sleek? What sort of people are your customers? What are they buying?

Whatever your vision is, this should become your 'true north' for making decisions about how you want your café to be. It will become your café's identity, your brand and your soul. A vision you are passionate about, that people can see and feel when they come to your café and even get excited about. It is going to be the thing that gets you through. Your vision needs to be bigger than just making money, it needs to be a statement about what you want to offer your customers and how you want them to perceive and experience your café. It should be an expression and extension of yourself.

### Petar:

*My vision was based around health, fitness and wellbeing, so as a result I made sure we reflected this throughout the business. Our food and drinks were wholesome, colourful and full of nutrition, with very little processed foods. Our staff were aligned with this and were young, vibrant and active. Some with personal training backgrounds and were able to offer customers fitness advice and exercise guidance also. We became known as the place to go for well presented, fresh and great tasting healthy food and drinks.*

*Not only did this reflect in our customer base, but eventually in the street itself as well. As businesses around us were closing down, they were replaced with personal training, massage and yoga studios. After speaking with the owners I discovered the association and popularity of our business in the health market was a factor in attracting them.*

13

### The business plan

**Ben:**

*A business plan is a living, breathing document. I was approached a few times to mentor people starting a business and was asked about my business plan. I had to answer that I didn't have one. In fact, I did – it was just in my head, not on paper. However, you should do as I say, not as I do, and I would suggest you develop one. A business plan is no guarantee that things will work, but it will help to keep you on track while creating your business. It helps you to achieve each goal, to monitor and redefine your goals, and to modify and grow your business. It includes your market research, competitor analysis, strategy, risk analysis and mitigation, budget and review processes.*

You can use the topics in this book as a guide for your business plan. We have included a template on our website for you to follow. Primarily you need to write everything in as much detail as you can. You're already clear about why you're starting your business, now you need to answer - Who, What, Where, When and How.

**Review your business plan regularly. Break your long-term goals into achievable short-term ones. Focus on achieving these and occasionally review your long-term ones. It will help make day-to-day decision making easier and each small goal reached is one step closer to your business success.**

## Effective goal setting

As early as possible in your journey, get into the habit of setting goals. Goal setting will work in tandem with your business plan and vision. In order to take meaningful, purposeful action towards your vision you need to identify clear goals for you and your team to work towards in all areas of the business. Identify what your benchmarks are, and work backwards from there.

Break your goals into yearly, quarterly, monthly and weekly targets. Categorise them according to sales, marketing and operational initiatives. This way you know what you need to do and what your targets are on any given day and you can track and measure your progress. If you aren't setting your goals and reviewing regularly, you are essentially operating with guesswork and your results will reflect this. A good coach will be able to help you strategise and guide you on a plan for your business, as well as keep you accountable to stay on track.

Follow the S.M.A.R.T goal setting system. Ensure your goals are Specific, Measurable, Achievable, Relevant and Time-Bound. This way your goals will be detailed enough to know what you want to achieve, by when, whether you're on track, or what needs to be adjusted or reviewed. Doing this will give you the best possible chance to achieve your goals which in turn will lead to your success.

## Who are your customers?

Who do you envisage serving when you think about your café? If you are situated in the city, your main market will probably be businesspeople and your biggest seller coffee and quick meals. If in the suburbs, it is likely you'll get mum's groups and weekend breakfasts. You will be catering to your core group of customers however you will have many others who aren't in your target group who are also likely to come in.

The style of café you choose to operate is likely to dictate who you attract. Unless you are churning out coffees and food to the masses, production line style, you are likely to attract people who have a similar style and tastes to you.

That's fine if you have an awesome taste that appeals to a lot of other people just be very clear about who you see as your customer base. Think style, location, vibe and pricing. Who is likely to be in the area you plan to operate in? Tradesmen, business people, students, families, travellers and tourists?

### Ben:
*I had to laugh the other day as I walked past a Mother's group sitting on a blanket on the floor bouncing their babies on their knees. Two nights earlier I had three punk bands playing and jumping off the small stage. That's pretty random and I wouldn't have picked it but my day trade caters to business people, coffee drinkers and mum's groups to whom I sell hot chocolates and muffins. Going into the evening its beers, nachos and bands catering to the slightly alternative crew.*

## What are you selling?

Are you just selling coffee and food or are you selling an experience? Mums probably don't want fried food and trendy people probably don't want salad sandwiches or to spend time in your business and industrial takeaway. We go into menu design later in the book but give some thought to the type of food, service, quality and cost of what you plan to sell and does it match who you think your customer will be.

# Where is your café?

Once you have your business plan and a budget you can start looking for premises from which to run your business. Have you ever been somewhere that doesn't seem to feel right? Great concept, wrong area. To avoid your place feeling like this, you need to have the concept for your café in the forefront of your mind while you look for your premises.

If you plan on doing quick lunches and breakfasts then you want to be where the people are. Suitable locations include shopping strips, office buildings, and wherever there is a high density of people who want to eat. If you're doing takeaway, look at industrial areas, high-density areas or large shopping centres. If you want to open a lounge style you will be more likely to consider cool suburbs, back streets, areas near parks, the beach, or smaller strip shopping areas.

For a coffee only business, look at locations near major retail centres or office blocks, or possibly sub-leasing a small space inside gyms or bookstores. For a mobile coffee service, look at markets, festivals and events unless you plan to go door to door, business to business.

These aren't strict rules, as many cool cafés are situated in odd places. However, there is no point doing a takeaway inside a gym or a lounge in an industrial business park for example.

### Ben:
*I found an old building in an up-and-coming suburb. It lacked walk by traffic, but there was nothing else around that provided a lounge vibe so I created a destination that offered that.*

### Petar:
*My location was off the main road on a residential street with limited exposure and quite a few cafes in the area, but I saw a lot of potential in my vision and my point of difference. I felt if I created the right type of place we would attract customers and make it work.*

**Don't be put off if there are already lots of cafés in the area. That can be an advantage as it draws more customers. Just make sure you can create a distinct point of difference. Don't put too much focus on what other cafés are doing. Instead, concentrate on what you can do well.**

# When will your doors open?

Keeping a flexible time frame is crucial, as things don't always go to plan. Map out six months or even longer from the start of your project to your proposed opening date and write in key objectives. For instance, you'll need to consider organising or acquiring:

- A signed lease before you do any work
- Legal permits
- Furniture and decor (if you fit out from scratch)
- Equipment
- Suppliers and stock
- Staff
- Cooking utensils
- A launch party

The list goes on, but hopefully, you are getting the picture. While things rarely go to plan, with patience, flexibility and a proactive approach to problem-solving, things will eventually fall into place.

# How?

Well, it's your journey, and unless you're buying an established business or franchise it's up to you. Fortunately, the following chapters will assist you in the how.

**Check websites such as freelancer.com and Fiverr for opportunities to get your logo, branding, menu and any other design elements of your business done to a high standard for a reasonably low cost. You can review the portfolio of designers worldwide and choose who you want to work with.**

# CHAPTER 3
# TYPES OF BUSINESS MODELS

B y now you've got some idea of the type of business you want to run, but before you look at how to finance it, you need to consider what type of ownership set-up to go with. Do this now, because it will influence your financing.

## Owner-Operator

If you're going to be an owner-operator, make no mistake – you have bought yourself a job until you get to a stage where someone can manage it for you. Then you will have an investment. Until that time you will work like you never have before.

You'll be preparing food, washing dishes, cleaning floors and tables, restocking toilet paper, all those glamorous jobs you don't see when you sit down for your daily latte – as well as controlling and managing the business

There are benefits and difficulties to being an owner-operator.

The benefits include being your own boss. You aren't obliged to answer to anyone. What you sow you reap; all profits are yours, and your business will grow as you do.

The main disadvantage is that you are on your own. Financially, you're one with the business. You're directly responsible to suppliers. You will also have an enormous workload, especially at the start. You are the HR department, marketing, maintenance, payroll, accounts and workforce.

*Ben:*

*I had nothing to lose so I enjoyed being an owner-operator. However, at times I wished I had a partner in the business to enjoy the triumphs and share some of the load when times were tough.*

*Petar:*

*After many years in the structure of a corporate career, I enjoyed the responsibility of being an owner-operator and steering the direction of the business. I was directly responsible and accountable and liked the fact I didn't have to rely on anyone or ask for permission to make decisions. However, there were times when it did get somewhat lonely. I was working long hours and especially during those times we were quiet and there wasn't financial return for my efforts was challenging. Nobody in my immediate network owned a business so I didn't feel they could relate to my circumstances and I didn't share much with them. In hindsight, his could have been harmful to my mental health. My advice here is to find people you can engage with, learn and get support from – as well as offering the same. Your business grows as you do, so find ways to develop yourself and expand your own network, especially if you don't have any business owners or entrepreneurs to spend time within your current circle of family and friends.*

# Partnership (2-20 partners)

When a business is set up as a partnership, it means that the control and management of the business are shared, as are the profits and losses. Be sure to research the laws of your country and state to understand what legally constitutes a partnership.

The advantages of a partnership include having someone to share the financial burden and the workload. It's also nice to have someone to share both the good times and the bad times. And in the right partnership, you'll find the adage 'two heads are better than one' to be all too true.

But there's also a potential downside. You hear time and time again about fallouts, partners ripping each other off, or some other reason they fail. Relationships may not last, and it's a fact that when the pressure is on it increases the chance of them going bad. While this is common, so is the ability of some individuals to combine into an effective team.

*Ben:*

*I took on a business partner after nine years. I started with a couple of small business partnerships that were off-shoots in my café. While each of those dwindled, I never for a moment thought it was a waste of time as I did make money from them and learned valuable lessons each time.*

*My current business partner invested four years ago and today our partnership is working fine. Our start, however, was messy. He didn't come up with full payment, I still owed some money to the tax office, and I had traded as an owner-operator and ran everything as I wanted. This was quite confusing for him. It took a good twelve months and repeated conversations until we got everything running smoothly.*

*Communication and being able to get on the same page was a big issue. My business partner brought technical skills such as computing and setting up electronics. He was good at sourcing supplies and was amazingly well-informed about all sorts of things that didn't interest me. This left me more time to focus on the creative and visionary side of the business, which I enjoy and have a flair for.*

### Petar:

*I started off alone, then after some months of consistent growth was in a good position to introduce a partner. My wife was working full-time in a finance career but was keen to join me in this business. This decision was easy as our relationship was rock solid, communication was open and we already knew and trusted each other.*

*In addition to this, while my skills were in leadership, communication and the vision and direction of the business, my wife preferred to be a part of the team while overseeing the financials. Our skills complement each other perfectly and our business grew significantly when she came on board. It wasn't always perfect, but we had a strong enough relationship and partnership to navigate any challenges.*

*Introducing a partner can make or break your business, and compliment or clash with your skills and personal style. Be sure to understand how you'll be able to work together with any partners – especially during difficult times. Understand yourself, your personality and your own skill set, and then work out what type of partner you would need for your business.*

If you're starting up as a partnership, find out what each of you does well, delineate tasks and remain accountable to each other.

You also need to be clear about responsibilities and expectations before you start, and it may be worth putting these in writing. You will need to be clear down to the smallest details, including what you pay yourself, what constitutes a working hour, whether you pay for your food, what discounts you give to friends or family, among other things. Decide what to authorise each other to do and spend without consultation. The list is long, but you want to cover everything to save misunderstandings down the track.

You should also consider what might happen if one of you wishes to exit the partnership. This is crucial and should be detailed in your initial partnership deed. What if one of you passed away, where does the share go and what input does the beneficiary have? This could mean you have a new partner who may not understand your business. So how do you go about creating a partnership? This can be as simple as buying into an existing business or creating one with others.

It is critical to consult a legal professional for advice and to formalise any paperwork for a partnership and conditions you wish to include. A partnership can be as detailed as you like or as simple as a handshake, however, the latter leaves everything open to each partner's interpretation and would likely end in grief.

Partnerships can be very fruitful, but make sure you cover every base before entering one.

**Discuss which business model suits your position with your accountant from the outset. This will save you restructuring your business at a later date which will cost more money.**

# CHAPTER 4

# FINANCING YOUR VENTURE

T here are a number of different ways to finance your venture. We discussed earlier how we budgeted and financed our businesses. However, you decide to finance your venture, get advice from your accountant. These options are based on Australian culture and knowledge, but they can be applicable elsewhere.

## Banks

Small business finance is the hardest to secure. Unless you have equity in property or someone willing to go, guarantor, you probably won't be able to get a bank loan, they won't want to know you until you've shown good profits for a couple of years.

## Friends

Be wary of borrowing from friends or family as this has been the cause of many good relationships going sour.

### Ben:

*I lent $25,000 to help some friends in a property deal that went bad. It was just bridging the gap for one week but it took eighteen months before I saw my money again. If you do borrow from friends or family make sure they are aware of the risk and that if things go bad it may take some time to get their money back. And even though you're friends, it's a good idea to put something in writing.*

## Using equity

As for borrowing against your own property, make sure that if you draw on it that you won't be in jeopardy of losing your home. Business is a risk, a calculated one perhaps, but a risk nonetheless so only risk what you can afford to lose.

# Savings

If you have a long-term dream to start a café why not start saving now and get as much money in the bank while you formulate your plan. This may only serve part of your start-up or could serve as emergency funds.

## Superannuation/Retirement Fund

Not the greatest capital to gamble with, and remember there is no guarantee of success be wary of using your retirement benefits. Ben drew on a portion at one point as business expanded but get some financial advice prior to considering this as an option.

# Making do

If you're cash-strapped and have a good credit rating you can lease or hire-purchase equipment and furniture. Sometimes you can get by with some domestic equipment until you can afford the proper industrial grade machines. Some items you cannot afford to skimp on such as a good coffee machine and grinder.

If you ever get a call from someone to book an appointment to discuss business equipment deals, be very wary. You'll see in Chapter 16 "Scams and rip-offs" that there are numerous unscrupulous people and organisations that will take your money. Do your sums and do your research. Ben was stung close to $30,000 over five years for equipment that went out of date very quickly.

**To save some set-up costs consider starting with domestic appliances taking advantage of interest-free terms from large appliance stores. Check warranty terms as you are using them for commercial purposes. Assess what you'll be using it for and make an informed decision as to whether it can withstand its purpose. Some domestic equipment and appliances can be suitable and last years. Be aware, as you must pay it off before the interest-free period ends or you end up paying very high interest on the whole amount not just what is outstanding.**

# Investors

If you're prepared to give away some of your business and have the right people on board, you can look for investors in your business. Be clear on the level of involvement, as with partnerships. Seek clear legal and accounting advice before using other people's money.

# Crowdfunding

Kickstarter and GoFundMe are examples of crowdfunding platforms. If you have a vision that is compelling and people can see value in it, then crowdfunding may be a potential source of startup funds. This forum is becoming increasingly popular so if you have the idea and can sell it, have a look.

# CHAPTER 5
# BUYING A BUSINESS

It's difficult to know exactly how much capital you need to start a new business, but you can avoid that problem altogether by purchasing an existing business. We'll delve further into what you will have to consider when building your own business from scratch later, but first let's take a look at what's involved in buying an existing food business.

## Franchises

Everything is set out for you to walk in and start. Marketing, policies and procedures; everything is in place for you. All you need to do is pay for it and pay ongoing percentages as dictated by that franchise. The downside of buying a franchise is that it can be costly, as you are paying for knowledge and support, and you're restricted in what you can do and sell.

Buying a franchise can potentially be a good way to go if you're looking for an investment, or a straightforward way to enter the industry. If this is what you want and you can afford it, your chances of success can be higher in a proven and established brand. The set-up will be structured; however, you will still need to consider other issues such as staffing, scams and personal development.

Be sure to be very thorough in your research of store and business performance, the brand itself and whether it's a fit for what you're looking to achieve. Entering into the wrong franchise partnership can end in financial disaster, however the right one can be very fruitful.

## Independent businesses

Be careful when buying independent businesses. Unlike a franchise, there are no guarantees of what structures are in place. There is no support network unless you know other people in business, no marketing plans designed by the corporate head office, no HR and no training department. Just you and the connections you'll make in the future.

Even the highest level of due diligence is no guarantee of success. You may be just buying someone else's headache. If you're considering buying someone else's business, you should ask some important questions.

# Can I afford it?

Generally speaking you should expect your investment back within three years. A basic calculation for buying an Australian business is: **Yearly profit x 3 + the value of stock + goodwill.**

Stock should be calculated at wholesale price, but also take into consideration stock you're planning to sell. If there are items you don't wish to sell, such as packaged goods and promotional items that you don't intend to continue with, then they aren't worth anything to you so shouldn't be included in the equation.

Some accountants will advise you that goodwill is worth nothing. However, if everyone knows that a number of apartments are going up and the area is developing, for example, there may be some goodwill worth calculating.

# Why are they selling?

You can ask this question, but you might not want to take the answer at face value. Our advice would be to take the week off and sit in the café to see what happens. You can observe operations and get to know who you might want to retain, at least in the short term.

# Can I maintain or make this business better?

If it ain't broke, don't fix it. Make sure you'll be comfortable running the business as it is, at least for a while. It's beneficial for you to retain any staff initially. Discuss your intentions with the staff as soon as you know you're going to take over. Many people are not comfortable with change, and this could prevent a mass evacuation.

Take your time to understand how the business works, who the customer base is, and what other things they might like. If you think you can make it better, don't rush in and change everything – furniture, design and menus – only to have a grand opening and be out of business in three months because you spent all your money on doing the place up.

Loyal customers mean you have money coming in the door from day one, and you want to retain them and the income they provide. They can also be wary of change, so introduce any changes you make gradually. These changes should be focused on building and expanding relationships as well as increasing efficiency or quality in the business that creates value for your customer and value to you in the long run.

### Ben:

*My cousin opened a successful sandwich bar. It was the only one in the area, but when he sold it the new owners closed it down and renovated at great expense. The new business survived for a while before it was sold again for a substantial loss. They made some of the biggest mistakes, including not understanding the location or the market and investing heavily on changing a well-performing business.*

*If the style of business you envision is nothing like the one you're considering buying, it might not be for you.*

## Is everything owned by the business and included in the sale?

Don't assume that everything you see at the café belongs to the business. Get an inventory of exactly what is included in the sale. Also, don't pay for something you don't need. Many items are expensive and can be leased for tax benefits, so it might not be worth buying them. Some items are owned by suppliers who impose certain conditions on the business. You should also check what equipment is or isn't under warranty, as hospitality equipment is expensive to repair.

### Petar:

*Upon selling my business, we outlined specifically what was included in the sale with prospective buyers. This included everything from stock on hand (coffee, packaging, produce, etc.), to a television and an iPhone used for orders. We also informed buyers what was on lease, so they could choose whether to enter their own contract for appliances and machines or for us to cancel those. Communication is key, and if the seller isn't being transparent or is withholding information, consider that a red flag.*

## How long is the lease?

Assuming you're buying the business only, you'll want to know how long the lease is. Make sure you're not buying a business that could be closed down soon or subject to re-negotiation and a likely rent increase.

***Petar:***

*A good lawyer is crucial in reviewing the lease documentation. I engaged a lawyer who I paid to review documentation, and he was a referral from someone close to me. It seemed like he did the right thing and we signed the lease and opened our business.*

*It wasn't until we were looking at selling years later that we discovered some vital conditions that were overlooked and this had an impact on our sale price. Firstly was the length of the lease. As I didn't have any experience and didn't know where to turn for support, I assumed the lease was a reasonable length. Unfortunately I discovered it was on the shorter side which left prospective buyers even less time in the property under the current agreement. I attempted to renegotiate but the landlord declined.*

*Another condition was a "Demolition Clause". The landlord could effectively give us 6 months notice and then choose to demolish the building. The lawyer did not bring this to our attention, and it significantly devalued our business. Be wary!*

*Be very thorough in who you engage as an advisor, not just lawyers but accountants and other services. It can be the difference between saving you a lot of time and money, or ending your business aspirations.*

# What are the neighbours like?

After taking over a business, introduce yourself to nearby businesses and find out what they think of your purchase and what they might like to see happen to it. It will help you to provide a better service and may identify areas of the business that you can grow, but don't take every single thing as gospel or deviate from your vision.

***Ben:***

*I have people coming in asking for something we took off the menu nine months ago because it wasn't selling. They tell me how good it was and how it should be back on the menu. I smile and thank them for the compliment, and suggest that if they visited more often I might just consider it.*

# Independent business checklist

There are benefits to buying an existing business as most of the work is done, but there are still risks, and you should try to mitigate these. As well as asking the questions listed here, make sure that you do due diligence on the paperwork. Items to check include:

• Ask why the owner is selling.
• Ask for a profit and loss statement (from their accountant).
• Ask for a balance sheet (for your accountant).

- What sort of lease is in place? Talk with the agent or owner to confirm details.
- Ask for an inventory of stock.
- Ask for an inventory of equipment, brand, and service history.
- Ask if the business owns the equipment.
- Is there any equipment still under finance?
- Are there any outstanding debts to suppliers?
- Get a list of suppliers and call them up to ask how their relationship has been.
- Make sure all permits are in place and current. Check with the appropriate council.
- Who is their insurance with?
- Are they prepared to stay on for a transition period as you take over?
- Out of the staff, who is likely to stay and go?
- What parking is available for you, your staff and customers?

Without badgering the person selling find out as much as you can and be aware that some of these conversations are in confidence. Respect that they don't wish to make staff or customers nervous.

If you are going forward with buying a café, do your due diligence and get a full picture of what you're investing in.

**If you buy an existing business, make sure a clause is added to prevent the current owner from setting up a similar business within a certain time frame and distance from the one you're taking over.**

# CHAPTER 6

# LOOKING FOR YOUR SPACE

If you don't want to buy an existing business, you'll have to find suitable premises and start from scratch. This can be especially exciting and rewarding. We talked earlier about picking a good location, now let's look more closely at the building itself. Once you've located premises that you think might be suitable, call the real estate agent to get a look inside.

Below are some items you might want to consider when looking at a potential site for your business.

• Size – can you operate within this space? Think of the space you need for kitchen, bar, servery, and customers.

• You will more than likely make changes to it; think about how difficult this will be.

• Consider disability access to the premises.

• Does the venue have the power capacity required for commercial equipment? A lot of hospitality appliances, such as larger coffee machines, require a higher output and as your need increases you may have to upgrade the power supply. You don't necessarily need it as power points can be converted; however, it's good to know in case you buy bigger equipment in the future.

• Check the water – is it hot, cold and clean?

• What is the floor covered with?

• Where are current power points and lighting positioned?

• Check the locks and condition of all windows and doors.

• How many toilets are there?

• Can a toilet be converted for disability access?

• What is the natural light like?

• Are there any noise factors – major roads, train/tram lines (you can tell - we're from Melbourne) that could impact your business?

• Is there public transport nearby?

• Does the premises have its own parking? What street parking is available for customers?

• Is there room for kerbside tables or outside dining?

• Is painting required?

• What hours do surrounding businesses keep?

There is a lot to check out! Keep notes and take photos. Bring a friend or two who have good attention to detail; they may see things you don't. Make yourself a checklist and give them a copy to go through
and go back as many times as necessary.

Please don't rush finding your venue for fear someone else will snap it up. What will be will be. We both looked at and missed out on places until we walked into the one that felt right and got the necessary approvals.

### Ben:
*Subsequently I discovered that one of the premises I missed out on did become a café. Unfortunately for the owner it was out of business in a year, and it would never have been big enough for what transpired in my business.*

# Leasing
As well as everything in the list on the previous page, there are some extra items to consider if you're planning on leasing the property.

• How much is the rent? Make sure you find out whether taxes and outgoings are included.

• What are the outgoings? Under a commercial lease you either directly or indirectly pay for the landlord's costs, which include all amenities, rates and insurance.
• How long is the lease? Will the landlord give you a few months free or reduced rent for a period to set up? Keep in mind you will be improving the property.

• What amenities are available?
• Are there any restrictions on what you can do?

If you aren't buying the property, you need to know that (in Australia at least) commercial tenancy agreements favour the landlord as opposed to domestic tenancies that favour the tenant.

Seek to ascertain whether the owner is looking for a long-term tenant. A long-term lease is recommended, as this allows time to build the business, and if you choose to sell you have a lease available for the incoming party.

### Ben:
*I started with a 3x3x3, renegotiated an extra three-year term after the first lease expired, and after twelve years I negotiated a further 15 year lease.*

# Subletting
Subletting part of your space may be an option while growing the business if you have the capacity. You can look at businesses and pop-up shops which compliment yours. We cover this in more detail in 'Chapter 18 - Diversifying'.

It's important to ensure that you're able to sublet under the terms of your current lease, even if you don't think you will need to. You never know how things are going to change, and trying to amend your lease in the future will cost you and the landlord may not be open to it. It's best to have flexibility so the business can adapt with changing circumstances.

### Ben:
*I started out leasing space to therapists, but I only charged commission. This isn't officially subletting but more renting space on a casual basis. A better option would have been tying them into a contract and making them commit.*

If you sublet, make sure you create a rental agreement with clear terms. Rental agreements can be downloaded from the internet. Make sure it is from the appropriate authority for the area you operate in.

If you have the space available, consider subletting. Ben made the mistake of renting both storeys of a whole building rather than growing into the second storey. This cost him an extra $40,000, which could have been subsidised by subletting until he was ready. If you're looking at a large space at least make sure you can sublet part of the property while you get established.

# CHAPTER 7

# COUNCILS, PERMITS AND INSURANCE

B efore you can fit out your café the way you want you will need to visit and enquire with the appropriate authorities (whether it's your local council or other law authority in your area) and if you're renting you should do this before you have a lease drawn up.

This is where you should seek information about building and planning permits, health regulations, disability access, and liquor licencing permits.

Here is a list of just some of the permits and licences you may need. This differs between councils, states, territories and countries:

• Building and planning permits – this is a one-off, but get it right the first time as you pay every time you want to make changes.

• Building survey for capacity of patrons (one-off)

• Health or food service certificate (annual fee)

• Food handling certificates for yourself and staff (one-off; see Chapter 19 - Training)

• Liquor licence (annual fee)

• Responsible Service of Alcohol certificate (renewable annually)

• Permit for outside dining (annual fee)

• Signage and a-frame permits, may be linked to the above (annual fee)
• Licences and approvals that regulate the playing of music in a commercial venue.

Before you visit your local authority you will likely need plans of the premises and the design of your café, including floor layout, patron capacity, location of fire exits, fire extinguishers and possibly more. By providing as much information as you can in the beginning you will reduce your visits and time spent.

In most countries, to get your planning permit you will need drawings of your proposed layout, but things may change as you go. To save money, try to draw to scale and with accuracy on the first attempt. You should have plans from the previous owner or landlord to start you off, and if you have a friend who is good at graphics ask them for some help. The initial drawings don't have to be professional, but you will need to show clearly where your equipment will go, where the exits are, which way doors swing, etc.

This is also where you start spending money. If you're renting, don't sign the lease until you have your planning permit. A signed lease is in place for years and there is no use having premises without having a permit to operate in it.

**Look for a project management book for beginners that will help plan tasks, timelines and responsibilities to keep you on track.**

# Dealing with your local Council

*Ben:*
*I got so frustrated with the council that I almost stopped before I started. I was dealing with the health department and the planning department and finding things out as I went. The planning inspector denied approval because my fire hydrant was one centimetre too low and my disabled toilet support bar was slightly out too. I had rebuilt the toilet because a wheelchair couldn't fit in and had bought the bar for the wrong side but installed it anyway, as well as the correct bars. He was pulling me up for the one that wasn't even meant to be there!*

*Tip: bite your tongue as much as possible. He let me off in the end but you could have guessed what was aching to come out of my mouth.*

*If you know my place you'll know the streetscape was lacking. I was warned by a Council Officer from another department who had a reputation for being a bastard about my chairs,* *tables and umbrellas out on the footpath. We had excessive space that was more than enough to allow people to pass. When I proved that it was fine with a measuring tape, he then changed tack and said the style of my tables didn't fit in with the streetscape. What @#\*% streetscape, I was creating it! Eventually I opened my courtyard and moved my tables inside and saved on outdoor furniture fees.*

What you need to understand is that councils have different hands, and while one is encouraging and helpful (as long as you stick to their specifications), the other hand is ready to wield the big stick and hit you with fines. You'll never get them on your side if you argue, so it's best to remain pleasant at all times. If you feel you have been hard done by, ask to speak to the supervisor. Remember also that your time is money, so it may not be worth fighting. Pick your battles. You can outsource obtaining some of the permits to other people rather than managing the process yourself. It will save time but will cost you money.

**Try to envisage the hours you will operate in the future. You need not keep these hours from the outset, but you can always extend them at a later date.**

### Ben:
*I never foresaw that I would work past 5pm so I had to extend my hours twice; first to 11pm and then again to 1am. This cost me a few extra thousand dollars for council permits and liquor licences.*

# Insurance
Insurance is a whole field in itself. And it's important to get your insurance organised before you open – you don't want to have a fire on the opening night and curse yourself for not having 'got around to it' yet.

If you are leasing your premises, depending on where you're from you will possibly need the following insurances:

• Public liability insurance

• Loss of business

• Loss of income

• Fire

• Theft

36

• Accidental damage

• Plate glass (even though you don't own it you'll be responsible for breakages)
• Worker's compensation

If you plan to buy rather than lease, you will also need to cover your standard building insurances that you pay regardless as it is built into your outgoings.

For more information about insurance, contact an insurance broker. Generally, if they're any good they should know which companies give the best value for your money. If you don't know a broker, start with your accountant, as they should have someone they can refer you to.

THE CAFE GUYS

# PART 2
# LET'S GET STARTED

# CHAPTER 8

# FITTING OUT YOUR CAFÉ

Y ou've got your vision, you've got your finance, you've got your business arrangements in place, the lease or title has your name on it, and the council has signed off on the permits. Now comes the really exciting part – walking through the door and picking up the tools to make your vision a reality.

Your first tools will be a pencil, paper and measuring tape. Sketch, plan and make notes of what you saw in your visualization from Chapter 2. Where are people sitting? Are there benches at windows? Where are you storing equipment and stock? What about the coffee machine and grinder, cash register, phone, cookie jars, tea canisters, glasses, wine, and so on? It will need to flow so you and your staff don't have to step over each other all the time.

Whatever you draw now, the chances are you will modify it again and again until you get it right. Don't get frustrated; be patient with yourself. Research other venues and use ideas that you can adapt and make your own. If you've got the capital, consider engaging a professional to assist you. Interior designers and architect firms can help with your concept.

If you think you can oversee the re-fit of your premises, then go for it, but many of you will want to hire a builder to organise the project. Use 'Pinterest' and 'Google Images' to create a photo board while doing your research. Otherwise take pictures of things you like, and copy pictures you see in the media or online.

# Builders and tradespeople

By now you'll be working on a number of different projects to do with building your cafe at the same time. You will be working with authorities, advisors and looking at fitting your place out. You will also be looking for tradespeople to build your vision, and possibly a builder to oversee the whole project. You need to be very clear and specific about what you want and know where you're prepared to be flexible. There are fantastic tradespeople who are creative and could contribute ideas, some of which might cost you more and some that will save money.

You're more than likely going to need a carpenter/cabinet maker, plumber and electrician. You might need people to work on windows and locks if you're changing those, as well as a sign writer and painter.

You can locate these people during the planning stage. If you don't know any tradespeople, ask friends and family for recommendations. Visit cafés that have fit-outs that you like. Ask who they used and if they would mind giving you a contact number. Word of mouth is a very effective method, but ensure you follow up with your own research.

You'll want to create good relationships with your tradespeople as you're likely to need them again; quite possibly in an emergency.

### Petar:

*I engaged an interior designer about 12 months into my venture in order to redesign and maximise the space, creating a fresh new look. I relied solely on a referral from a very nice and well meaning customer who has owned a number of successful cafes and he had worked with her previously, speaking very highly of her. Unfortunately, while her concept was great and she was on the same page as me and easy to work with, we were unable to act on much of her plans due to different planning and access restrictions, as well as landlord resistance. I was of the assumption that an interior professional wouldn't make recommendations that couldn't be implemented, or would suggest what permissions were required first. Also when asked by the local council to submit plans, they were surprised to find that there were no measurements on the plan either. This is the first and only designer I ever engaged and didn't research any others, so I'm not sure if this is a common and accepted practice or whether it was my own ignorance. Either way, ensure you're doing your research before spending your money on something that you may not even be able to put into practice.*

### Ben:

*Get quotes in writing. Work has a habit of blowing out in time and money. Many times I had tradespeople turn up without parts they needed even after seeing the job and quoting. They then charged me for time to go and source them. Unless there is some exceptional issue that arises there should not be any extra charges. Make sure GST or appropriate tax for your country is included in the quote.*

# Decoration and furniture

You can start looking out for decor and furniture while in the planning stage.

You might find things in unexpected places; some things may be in a large mainstream store and others may be a random opportunity. Auction houses and second-hand stores have chairs and tables that could suit your business. There are auction houses that have specialty hospitality auctions, but also go to office auctions as they often have large lots of near-new items that may fit your business.

Depending on your style, opportunity shops, major stores and bulk furniture stores are all worth a look. There are companies that specialise in hospitality furniture. If you do an internet search some are sure to come up. Always check online for savings, especially local classifieds and advertisements. Here you can find businesses who are renovating or upgrading and looking at selling their old stock cheap or even giving it away just to make room.

If you happen to notice or hear about a business that's closing, approach the owner and make an offer on any of their furniture and equipment that would suit you. It's sad for them, but every dollar they can make from items they no longer need will be helpful to them and save you a lot more. An auction house will take a premium to sell their unwanted furniture.

Buying new or made-to-order furniture will obviously cost you more than second-hand. What is appropriate depends on your design and what you're trying to create.

### *Ben:*

*In the months it took me to build I started buying bits and pieces whenever I saw something. I bought sixteen high-back lounge chairs from an auction for an average of $30 a piece. They had been imported from Portugal and were valued at $250 each. I hired a storage shed to keep everything in and just transferred it to the café when I was ready.*

*Keep a notebook, iPad or phone with you at all times. Take notes and photos of what you saw, where you saw it and the price. If it's a large supplier ask if they regularly stock the item. If they do, leave it for now as you might see something more suitable or better priced later. If it's a one-off item and you can definitely use it, buy it. I bought a piano for a steal at a second-hand furniture store I noticed while driving around. I did a deal on some old lounges and the piano on the spot. I went retro as it was cheap and suited the style I wanted. I was creating a*

41

*lounge and used 70s tables and chairs like mum and dad or your grandparents had, which made many people identify and connect to my place as soon as they walked in.*

*While I was putting my deposit down the phone rang and a lady who had wanted the piano and gone away to think about it missed out by minutes.*

*I also recently renovated my courtyard and required a dozen outdoor stools for a bench I created. I saved sixty per cent by searching online for the same stools I saw in a shop. Try to avoid the 'I have to have it now' mentality when shopping for your business. Go to hospitality auctions. They're a great place to pick up bargains if you cannot afford new equipment. Just remember you won't get a warranty – so choose carefully!*

# Lighting and colour

The colour scheme and the lights you choose dramatically affect the vibe of your place. There are so many cool things you can do with lighting; it can make your place look cool or warm, larger or smaller. It's worthwhile investigating the best lighting for your place.

Remember that if you have the best coffee, ravioli or some amazing dish, people will get over whatever colour your walls are. If you want them to hang around for hours and have a few drinks, then you really do need the atmosphere to encourage that. Lighting is part of that atmosphere. Consider what clientele you will have too, if you have people conducting meetings you may need to consider the ability to brighten the space at certain times.

Consider getting a professional decorator to give you some ideas, or if the budget is an issue, try approaching design students in their final year (it looks great on their resume).

### Ben:
*I used a lighting designer once for some exterior work, but it was a waste of my money as the owner wouldn't let me do what the designer initially suggested. I should have stopped there, as the designer did the next best thing that was a sub-standard second best. I have also had non-professionals with an interest in lighting make some suggestions that were really helpful. It doesn't hurt to ask around.*

*Also my business partner bought these great light bulbs that allow you to change the colour and brightness. We had clear instructions that at night we wanted them red as it sets a better vibe and makes people more attractive after a few drinks (that's a joke). When they were blue the place was bright and cold. The red gave the feel of intimacy and made you feel like having in-depth discussions in the corner, the blue like you were in a nightclub. Lighting is important.*

# Equipment

**Ben:**
*When I first started out, I remember having a conversation with a fellow named Steve – a friend of a friend who had agreed to help me out a bit and give me some pointers.*

*Steve was awesome. He had started and sold businesses and was a consultant who gave me his time for free. I distinctly remember showing him some plans. I already had my lease set up, was painting walls, and had a list of things I needed.*
*Then he asked me, 'So where are you going to get your cutlery?'*

*I just looked at him blankly and thought 'Hell, I need cutlery!' An important detail, but it hadn't*
*crossed my mind, and it still makes me laugh that I hadn't considered what people were going to eat with.*

So, what will you need? Again, the style of café and the range of food and beverages you'll be serving will determine the plates, cutlery and equipment that you will need.

With this in mind we have provided a general list, which is certainly not complete, but should give you a good start of things to consider.

- Coffee machine
- Grinder
- Cash register
- Juicer/Blender
- Ovens
- Toaster/sandwich press
- Printer
- Security/Video monitoring system
- Freezer
- Tables
- Chairs
- Shelving
- Fridge(s) (including display fridges)
- Glasses/Cups/Mugs/Teapots
- Plates, dishes and cutlery
- Dishwasher
- Sound system
- Serving utensils

- Ice machine
- Salt & pepper grinders
- Food thermometers
- Bathroom products (toilet paper, paper towels, soap)
- Mop/Broom/Vacuum/Cleaning equipment
- First aid kit
- Safe
- Assorted tools

You don't have to have everything to begin with, but there will be certain items that you will absolutely need.

There are many hospitality stores that have a significant range of good quality products. They will give you a trade discount but still may not be the cheapest option. Always look out for very inexpensive good quality items.

### Ben:

*As I started in an area with a strong Asian influence there were plenty of discount shops. I found some excellent, very cheap plates; seventy-five percent cheaper than a major store. They were branded, but not in the box. Cutlery can also be cheap, which I'd recommend you look at if you aren't going for higher-end dining. Auctions will always have a sale of mixed items that would go cheap; it's worth keeping an eye out.*

# CHAPTER 9

# WHAT'S ON THE MENU?

Your menu is going to depend on numerous factors such as demographic, style of café, kitchen facilities and staff abilities.

## Demographics

What style of café are you opening? Is it a sandwich bar, takeaway or eat-in? Is it a lounge or food store? Who are your customers? Your demographics will be a major dictator of what you serve. If you're in an industrial area with early morning starters, you're likely to need egg and bacon sandwiches, pies and other quick snacks for during break time. A selection of fresh sandwiches will be good sellers. If you're in an office block maybe your focus will be focaccias, soups and salads for lunches. An inner suburbs location would draw customers with a trendy space and menu to match. People get sick of the same thing so where possible change your menu regularly.

### Ben:

*I have tried it all: breakfasts, toasted sandwiches, baked potatoes, fresh juices, lentil dahl, veggie burgers, steak sandwiches, soups, salads, wraps, focaccias, pasta, freshly baked muffins, biscuits and cakes. I had the motto of whatever we do, we do it well. Not as easy as it sounds. Coffee was important to me, but everything we served had to be made correctly. With this in mind, and after I learnt I couldn't do everything, I kept adjusting my menu until I found the best combination of popular items. As a result I had minimal wastage and rarely threw out food (which is like throwing out money).*

### Petar:

*I started my business with a very small menu, and no hot food items at all. Our choices were essentially coffee, tea, protein balls, healthy treats and smoothies, and fresh salads and sandwiches which were prepared in the morning. There were no hot breakfasts or lunches and very little made to order food items. I did this intentionally for 3 key reasons. Firstly, to create a simple and easy to operate set up while I got used to the business and got experience with what was going to be expected of me in this venture. Secondly, to gauge opportunity and customer volume from what we were offering - a health based alternative to regular cafes and fast food options - and to understand how many employees I may need instead of hiring too many people I didn't need. Finally, anything done in the business I wanted to be of the best possible quality and standard. This meant getting familiar with a smaller menu and making it of a consistently high standard and then growing based on capacity. I didn't want to do too much too soon in a new business that I had no experience in, risk quality being compromised and customers have a negative experience which results in a bad reputation from the start. People talk and word travels fast - even faster now with social media. Instead I got the basics really well established, built a good reputation for quality and consistency and grew from there. In the years that followed we introduced breakfast and lunch options which were very well received and our business continued to grow and evolve. However, our rate of growth never exceeded my ability to maintain a high standard of quality and consistency.*

## Produce

What is available when? Restaurants and cafés have seasonal menus for a reason; fruit and vegetables are cheaper when they're in season. Some fruit becomes very expensive when out of season. However, also make sure you can source all your produce consistently (We cover finding suppliers in Chapter 11). When designing a menu, remember that you need to provide the same product again and again and again. Why do you think the big food chains are so successful? It's a system: three pieces of gherkin, a meat patty that weighs exactly 100g, a portioned squirt of mustard, and so on.

## Pricing your food

Pricing food depends on many different factors including:

• The cost to make the food
• Competitor food prices
• What your customers are prepared to pay

## Costs to make the food

To work out your costs you need to work out every component to make a dish. This includes all raw materials, time of staff taken to prepare, overheads, energy and portion of rent down to the infinite degree.

Who has time to do that right? Well, luckily those who have gone before have taken the time to develop tools that save you time. A rough costing is easy to achieve but depending on the complexity of the dish it may take more effort.

Costing your food won't always dictate what you can charge but it will show the minimum you must charge if you are going to make a profit from it.

### What's the cost of a sandwich?

Let's break it down to find out what your input costs are for an individual product you will sell.

Large bread roll – 1
Butter – 5g
Ham – 3 slices
Cheese – 2 slices
Lettuce – 50g
Tomato – ½ medium
Mayonnaise/mustard – 5g

*You have to cost each portion*

It takes one staff member 5 minutes to produce and 5 minutes to sell and package/serve. So 10 minutes in total, 1/6th of an hours wage (including superannuation).

You have a proportion of refrigeration, lighting, water for dish washing, insurance and premises to make it in. Breakages, equipment costs and wastages also need to be calculated. This is best calculated from annual bills and broken down to daily expenses.

Once you have these figures you will need to look at the total cost for the product. We can only guide you; however, a good rule is to aim for 100% markup.

The only exceptions you should consider are those items that support the sale of another product or those that may not have that percentage return but still yields a substantial profit. An example is you make 500% markup on a coffee but after costs it translates to $2 profit. However, you may sell a coffee mug that only has a markup of 75% and make $4 profit. It costs more to produce but less effort to sell for a better profit. It's important to remember that at the end of the day you are making a living - your lifestyle is paid for in dollars, not percentages. Keep this in mind when working out what you will be selling and their price points.

# Competitor food prices

While you shouldn't necessarily focus too much energy on your competition you should be aware of what the people around you are charging. If customers are paying a premium at your place, what are they paying for? The service? The ambience? The quality of your coffee and food?

You need to consider the differences in what you are offering, consider your costs and obviously what customers are prepared to pay. At the end of the day, don't be afraid to make a statement about what you are offering with your prices.

For example, if you want to make the cheapest sandwiches in the area, what is going to allow you to achieve this? Fewer overheads for a start. So maybe this requires you to be in a cheaper venue that may be less visible to foot traffic, in order to keep your overhead costs down. Then maybe your raw ingredients are going to be of a lower quality to reduce your input costs.

Alternatively you can purchase greater volumes, counting on attracting more people through the door of your café on the basis of lower prices. You are also going to have to minimise labour costs so this may mean preparing and wrapping sandwiches for customers to select and buy, rather than making to order.

You can see here there are a number of trade-offs to support your goal. You have to consider if being in a low traffic area will support this or act as a barrier. Good marketing could make you into a hidden gem if done well. This is just one example. Consider what your vision is and what variables you can compromise on and manipulate to your advantage.

# What your customers are prepared to pay

Competitor prices may give you a benchmark, but you also need to consider what your customers are willing to pay. Offering a high quality, highly serviced and expensive product, in an industrial area with people looking for quick and easy takeaway food, is obviously a mismatch to the demographic that the café is serving.

In the example below there are three different styles of café offering three different styles of product, each with different price points, competing for various types of customers and maybe some of the same customers on different days of the week.

48

**Joan's Cafe** is 'cheap and cheerful' but people go there for Joan who is a good character. Joan knows this, so she maintains prices for customer loyalty. $7.00.

**Gary's Gourmet** uses premium meats and rolls in his focaccia's and so charges extra accordingly. $8.50.

**Your Café** is new to the area, has a trendier look and feel to Joan's, but your product isn't of the same quality as Gary's. $7.00 is your bottom line so you might go $7.50 - $8.00.

If you are not experienced in running a kitchen, or not confident in creating the menu and pricing accordingly, hire someone who can. Knowing how much it costs to produce each dish is vital so you know what you need to charge at a minimum and how you can make things more cost effective.

Keep in mind – focus on what you can do well. Good service, good coffee, good food and you have the best possible foundation for your business.

### Ben:

*When I started the coffee prices were far lower than across town. I knew I was doing some of the best coffee in the area and I charged accordingly. Some local café owners would walk in to see what I was charging or ask when we met in the street. They would bring their price up without increasing quality. I would often have people come in and say we can get a mug of coffee for cheaper across the road to which my reply was 'By all means you are welcome to go across the road', as I knew their product was cheaper yet inferior. Within days they were back buying my coffee. You can stand by quality.*

**When designing your menu try to find more than one use for each item. For example, sliced ham can go on a baguette, in savoury muffins, on Eggs Benedict or in a baked frittata. This will reduce wastage and save money, so apply this to as many items as possible.**

## Staff abilities

Unless you run a full kitchen with professional cooking staff, keep it simple. There is no point trying to create a culinary masterpiece that only one employee is capable of making.

Only produce what you're capable of doing well and consistently. There is nothing worse than getting a dish you ordered only to find the ingredients aren't as described, it isn't properly prepared, or it's served incorrectly. Or ordering something at a cafe and having an amazing experience, then going back again and it's nothing like the last time you ordered. This is crucial in building customer loyalty.

You will need to test each dish you plan to put on your menu and show everyone how the recipe works. Bear in mind that some of the people you employ may not have made these dishes before, or even used some of the ingredients.

When you employ someone, whether it be for cooking or front of house, it's a good idea to ask them if they like cooking. See if you can incorporate their signature item or items into your menu without sacrificing anything else.

You may hit on a dish and could become renowned for it. You may have a barista who loves making cakes, so why not let them test their skills? You won't see an employee smile so much as when they were complimented for something they made.

Employees take more pride making something they know and love or have had input in than a dish that they don't understand or know how to make properly.

# Waiting and ordering

You need to consider abilities again depending on the type of service you are providing. Is it table or counter service? Waiting is a skill in itself and unskilled staff will need to learn how to deliver, clear and carry your dishes in the right manner and know how to conduct themselves around a table. If you offer table service, it's a great opportunity to sell customers another drink or something more. Be sure to understand this strategy and make sure your staff do as well. There are courses and books available on the topic and it can really boost your bottom line when executed consistently and effectively.

# Table service vs Counter service

Make it clear to customers as to how to order and where menus and cutlery are located if you aren't setting tables or delivering certain items. It's not a great feeling to walk into a place and wander around trying to work out how to get served, especially if staff are not as attentive as they should be.

***Petar:***
*I always tried to involve employees in decision making. By giving them input they feel valued, and also more invested in the business. This will translate into more care for the business and also a good morale overall as they feel a part of it, rather than simply being told what to do. Our staff members helped create menu items and because they felt valued, openly gave*

50

*suggestions to improve existing items - many of which were taken on board and either improved the quality of the dish or the efficiency of the item and menu.*

*To help with consistency we had an illustrated manual of how to prepare menu items. It specified which ingredients to use, measurements, and steps of preparing the dish, as well as pictures of how it should look. Not only did this help with consistency on a day to day basis, but also allowed new staff to learn faster.*

Menu choices should be limited to a selection of quality options. Too much on a menu makes it harder for a customer to choose. Make everything clear - where the menus are, how to order, how to get cutlery and water if not set on a table or delivered. Prices and signage should be clear so customers don't feel foolish. Also keep in mind staff recommendations are very powerful... we've all heard good service staff ask 'have you tried the...?' or of course the much more famous 'would you like fries with that?'

# CHAPTER 10

# COFFEE

C offee in its many permutations, is the lifeblood of a café. If you're opening a café make sure you get this part of your business right! It can be a lot of fun, and regular coffee drinkers can taste the love someone puts into their morning java.

## Coffee

**So what does it mean to serve quality coffee?**
The quality of coffee is in the result of the following equation:
• 25% the machine, including how well you maintain and clean it
• 25% the type, freshness, blend and roast of coffee bean
• 50% the ability of the person making it

The standards of coffee-making vary all over the world; however Australia has recently been doing extremely well in the World Barista Championships with a Barista from Canberra, Sasa Sestic, winning in Seattle in 2015. Australia placed 5th in 2017, 4th in 2014 and 2nd in 2013.

What does this mean? It means we know good coffee, but at the same time we shouldn't ever be complacent. Wherever you're from, whether there is a big coffee culture or not, coffee is consumed internationally, and you can build a reputation on this alone.

In this book we only skim the surface but it should be enough to get you going. If you intend to make special coffees such as cold press and use various methods of extraction you will need to do further research, but make sure you have the basics down first.

# The machine

Your machine will depend on what you can afford. A lot of coffee companies have deals with machine suppliers and can probably recommend something; they may even supply one provided you use their product. Your coffee supplier should be able to provide some training. You represent their brand, and they should want to help you make the best coffee you can.

The machine must be cleaned regularly, but as the chemical used is poisonous there are different theories on how often it should be done. It will depend on how much coffee you make, but start with your supplier's recommendation. The cleaning is a ritual, and when you get it right ensure your staff follow your lead. Keep a copy of cleaning instructions near your machine.

On a daily basis, as you're working, you should be flushing the group heads (you'll find out what these are) and wiping steam wands after every coffee. Milk stuck to the wands is burnt milk going off and tainting your coffee. It's a huge subject, but you'll learn all this through your training, whether through your supplier or otherwise, and as you become more experienced.

The machine should also be serviced regularly. We won't go into depth here, but it's like a car and some parts have more wear and tear than others.

# Coffee beans

Think warm and moist, and that's the climate where coffee grows. The birth place of coffee is Ethiopia, but it's grown in Asia, South America, mid to northern Australia, Papua New Guinea, all over Africa and everywhere in between.

There are two types of beans – Arabica and Robusta. Both beans provide a different flavour and will taste different on different parts of your palate. Beans will change slightly in character depending on altitude, temperature and humidity.

Robusta is more common, usually grown in lower altitudes, is faster growing and of the two beans is likely to be more bitter and less flavoursome. It is used to create depth and more crema in a coffee blend. Arabica is produced at higher altitude is slower growing, giving better flavours and is the feature of a good coffee.

Single origin means beans from one particular area.

Each area has its own flavour characteristics, and can also vary from farm to farm.

A blend is more than likely what you will use to begin with. If you're using a coffee company, this will be a major origin area where they can get volume. Boutique roasters, who aren't necessarily more expensive, will do small-batch roasting and probably have a lot more varieties.

## Roasters

Like a steak, you can create a recipe and cook a coffee bean to different levels of darkness which will change the flavour. Taste different roasts, with and without milk, and find which one you like. What you're looking for, assuming you'll start with only one blend, is a coffee that can please a short black drinker as well as have flavor through the milk to please latte drinkers. Hand that request to your supplier for now.

There are a variety of boutique, specialty and micro-roasters opening everywhere. There are large companies that everyone knows about, but also some new operators. Who do you choose? Go with the company that has the coffee you like, and that can also offer support and training. Having a good relationship with your supplier or roaster is crucial.

### *Ben:*

*I have changed coffee companies almost every three years for one reason or another. The first time was because I wasn't getting the support I needed; I was a small client to a big company. The second was because I couldn't get training when I needed it. I then went with a social enterprise company who changed terms on me even after I had set out what I wanted and the reasons for it. The last change was to a specialty roaster to create my own brand and blend.*

*One company I was with were great to deal with, but also supplied a nearby kebab shop and Vietnamese bakery who did the brand a disservice.*

## Coffee extraction

When you make a coffee you're actually extracting coffee oil from the bean. Your grinder breaks down the bean into granules, which are placed into a small basket. When placed in the machine the pressure and hot water forced through the ground coffee extracts the oil. This is the shot. There are standard shots, half shots, restricted and double shots, and they all have one or many names.

However, we do not wish to confuse or distract you with that right now. You will learn it.

This is where a barista's skill is evident. They can judge and adjust the grind to produce the best flavour out of the coffee bean. Throughout the day the grinder may need to be adjusted to allow for change in air temperature and humidity. Extraction is where the machine, grinder, roast and skill of your staff come together.

# Milk

Ever had a sip of a latte and burnt your mouth? It was probably about 80 degrees, way too hot and tasted like rubbish.

Technically you can't burn coffee, but when it tastes bad the culprit is often over-heated milk.

This is one of the reasons why, for milk-based coffees, handling the milk is as important as extracting a good shot.

Milk should be heated to between 60 and 65 degrees, bearing in mind the temperature will continue to rise even after you've stopped steaming.

The science works like this – building up the protein in the milk with steam creates froth. The fat in the milk breaks this down yet brings that creamy texture, silkiness and sheen. Different milk has different levels of protein, and this is why some froth better. Skinny or low-fat milk is easier to froth for this reason.

You'll need to decide which milk you want to use. A standard coffee is with full cream. If you have other milk available such as low-fat (skinny), soy, almond, rice or whatever, you can offer that too. I know purists who refuse to use anything other than full cream. That's fine as long as you have the customer base that allows you to do so.

With everything coffee-related, it is essential you get further training. Do a short course to get some basic information, skills and learn how to prepare and serve espresso. Learn to respect the art of making it however nothing is a substitute for practice.

# Tea

The tea industry is huge, and in the past few years some companies have taken it up a notch. I would suggest starting with the basic and most popular teas such as English Breakfast, Earl Grey, Chamomile, Lemongrass and Ginger, Peppermint and Green Tea.

Then choose a few different flavours…you name it there is something infused or blended with it. Orange, lemon, raspberry or juniper, it is endless.

What you do need to think about carefully is how you plan to serve it. In pots, in cups, in mugs? Try to pick one way that suits you and represents your style and business. Don't use mass produced supermarket purchased tea bags in pots. This type of tea in pots is okay when grandma makes it, but she's not charging up to five dollars for a serve.

Tea bags have gone high end too, so if you want tea bags check with what your supplier can offer.

# Hot chocolate

When we say hot chocolate, we aren't talking about Milo and warm milk. Chocolate is a specialty product that has made its way into cafés, and the cocoa bean is roasted much like the coffee bean. There are plenty of ways to make hot chocolate – powder, liquid, chocolate flakes, even chocolate fountains.

**Ben:**
*I make my own ganache, which is very basic but much loved and well known. Whatever you choose, do it well.*

# Chai tea/chai latte

'Can I have a chai tea, please?' is like saying 'can I have a tea tea please'. Chai or Cha is the word for tea in many countries around the world but in Australia it has come to take on the Indian meaning that is spiced tea (generally prepared with milk). There are a few types of chai, including loose leaf, powdered and syrups.

If you have the time, you can make it yourself with recipes readily available in cookbooks or online. Choose a method that works for you.

Chai latte is simply chai with milk. A popular method for making chai, and some will argue that it's the traditional, correct method, is to boil your tea and spices with milk. Most cafés don't have the time or space to keep a pot on the boil, so a quick method is to make a latte using a shot of chai as opposed to coffee. Add some cinnamon powder and honey as required and it's done.

# Other specialty hot drinks

In Australia, a number of other specialty hot drinks have been introduced and become part of a trend, for health reasons and otherwise, given their vibrant colours and unique ingredients. These include the tumeric latte, matcha green tea latte and beetroot latte to name a few. We suggest doing your own research and determining whether these will be worth introducing into your business and making a decision on if it is consistent with your brand and demographic. No point offering and stocking items and ingredients if they aren't being ordered.

# Latte art

If you have the time, the ability and it interests you … do it. After all, presentation is half the battle. Only do it when you've nailed the basics and you have the time. Just remember - no matter how good the art is, if the coffee isn't good you can say goodbye to your customer.

The basic floret and leaf will get you there or even a quick swirl with a toothpick. For drinks with chocolate or other specialty drinks, designs are easily and quickly added by making or buying a stencil to create a signature sprinkle on top of the drink.

### *Petar:*

*Earlier in the book I discussed how anything I did in the business, I made my mission for it to be at a high quality and standard. Coffee was no exception. I went into this venture with no hospitality experience, and this included no experience or knowledge about coffee. So I made sure I researched, learned and understood. Before getting our own coffee machine, while we were still in the planning stages, I did a one day coffee course. This was basically to familiarise myself with the equipment, terminology and give me a basic understanding of the coffee making craft.*

*From there I researched what coffee machine would best suit us and what volume we were predicting, as well as what beans and supplier to use. Fortunately I found a supplier who not only provided fantastic quality beans, but also cared about our success. They were essentially the full service provider of anything coffee related in our business. They provided a great coffee machine, 2 grinders (one for the standard blend and one for decaf) and serviced and maintained everything regularly. If there was a problem or repair required, I notified them and depending on the urgency they would send someone down - even within the day. Any repairs were at their expense. This price was factored into me committing to using their beans and assigned in the cost of the beans per kilo. As a result, the beans were a couple of dollars per kilo more expensive than other suppliers of a similar standard, but not having to pay for all the equipment needed as well as maintenance and repairs taken care of was great peace of mind.*

*In addition to this, they offered free training for staff as well as myself. This was great and ensured we were all on the same page, using the same process and making coffees the same way.*

*Once the machine was installed, I got to work practicing. The supplier gave me some free bags of coffee to start with and I used this to become competent in making the coffee. While planning and building my vision, I dedicated some time each day behind the machine and watching videos on YouTube. Learning how to adjust the grind for the perfect extraction, knowing how a good pouring shot should look like, what a good and bad coffee tastes like and smells like. Also, spending significant time with becoming competent in getting the milk right for lattes, flat whites and cappuccinos - the right amount of air, the right temperature, getting it spinning correctly. If you want to be successful in anything, no matter what skill it is, you need to be prepared to spend time practicing and getting all the details right. In hospitality, where any little complacency can result in a negative customer experience, a commitment and attention to detail is critical.*

**There are coffee tours in most cities and they are well worth the time and money to go for a walk and checkout some excellent operators. Try different coffees and styles - short black, long black, milk based, single origins. Notice what you like or don't like about them. This is especially recommended if you are new to coffee making.**

# CHAPTER 11

# FINDING YOUR SUPPLIERS

S o you're close to opening; the menu is designed, you've booked in for a coffee course, and now you need your produce, dry goods and disposables.

The menu naturally dictates what you need, but there will be core ingredients and you will more than likely need to find the following suppliers:

• A greengrocer or fruit and vegetable market
• Meat supplier or butcher
• Dry goods and frozen items
• Bakery for bread
• Paper suppliers for takeaway cups, packaging and toilet paper
• Coffee and tea supplier; most coffee companies do both but you may choose a specialty tea company.

It's good to go local if you can for freshness and fewer food miles but depending on the style of food you wish to serve you may be looking far and wide.

You can get most of your dry goods from one supplier, as most will carry everything from pre-sliced meats and serviettes to milkshake syrups and frozen products. Remember trade shows are a good place to source suppliers; however, the shows are infrequent so the internet is the best place to start these days.

There are plenty of suppliers. Ring a few and get their price list detailing all the lines they carry. You may find that you have options between two different suppliers. For instance, the milk supplier and provedore will probably both carry cream and sour cream. Choose your supplier on the quality and price range you prefer, but also keep the second supplier in mind in case of emergency.

Local farmers markets are also a great way to find suppliers, especially if you're looking for niche items for your café… a particular jam, bread or organic produce. Go online to find a directory of local community markets.

## Work smarter

Finding good suppliers is important, and the aim is to do as little running around as possible as your energy is needed elsewhere. Top chefs are down at the markets at 5am choosing the freshest and best ingredients.

However, as you'll be on your feet from as early as 5am making coffees or preparing for your day, you would most likely prefer to get most of your produce delivered to your premises.

### Ben:

*I struggled to get this across to my business partner when he joined me. I had managed to get my suppliers down to a fine art and, although I knew where I could make allowances and get better ingredients, I valued my time. Every hour I spent running around was an hour I wasn't getting paid and paying someone else to cover me.*

*My business partner could and did source some excellent products, but it took a better part of a year for him to realise how much time he was wasting running around. I have to admit at times I resented doing the running around when he wasn't able to.*

*I wasn't afraid to ask other cafés about their suppliers, or even enquire about a particular product they used in a dish. An experienced cook/chef should be able to recommend suppliers for most of the things you need.*

*I also go to every market I can as I often find great ideas and learn about cooking methods. These people are creative and you may spot something you like or can use.*

**Some suppliers charge fees or have a minimum order for delivery. They add up so work out your time versus money as sometimes it is worthwhile. Don't be afraid to negotiate as they want your business.**

# Paying the bills

**Your terms are basic.**

**COD:** Cash on delivery. Most new businesses have to start on this as they don't have commercial references yet. The longer you're around the more credible you are, and to be fair suppliers are the ones that are left out of pocket when businesses fail.
So while it's a hassle and inconvenient to start on cash, realise it isn't personal and once established you can call the shots. Remember that suppliers want your business more than you need their product. Unless they stock a certain specialty item, you can always find another supplier.

**Terms 14, 30, 60 days+:** Depending on the company, you can pay within any of these timeframes.

**Direct debit:** Just like your personal bills. Be careful with this; if your bank account gets overdrawn, banks will charge interest every time.

### *Ben:*
*You can pay by cash, cheque, credit or electronic funds transfer. I prefer EFT as I can track everything on my bank statement, but I occasionally use a credit card. To avoid any overdue fees, I'd use direct debit for anything that is leased or being paid off.*

*Check terms with your suppliers and be very clear if you wish to negotiate different terms. This will save you having accounts departments ringing you and asking where their money is. Many contracts state that the supplier can change the terms should they wish. Imagine if times get a bit tight, and the terms are changed from 30 days to 14 days or COD. Then the grief starts.*

*I travelled a lot and refused to use a supplier if I couldn't have 30 day terms. I didn't mind paying the first few deliveries COD, but after that I wanted to pay on account.*

*I had been with one supplier for nine years when they changed the terms on me. I had been a loyal customer for this whole time and was furious that they then started chasing me for money. I was tempted to dump them, but they were local and easy for me to get something quickly in an emergency. I decided not to cut them off just to prove a point .*

**Every dollar counts so set your terms and payment conditions to suit your needs and cash flow. Avoid extra bank fees by being aware of what comes out of your account and when... one bank fee saved just paid for this book.**

# CHAPTER 12

# STAFFING

It's a fact that hospitality is a transient industry. It attracts students, travellers, people on their way to somewhere else, and people who want a job to pay the bills while changing careers or pursuing their art or music. Apart from cooks, chefs, professional waiters and baristas very few people make hospitality a lifelong career.

## Sourcing staff

### Walk-ins

By far the best method we have found for sourcing staff is putting a sign in the window. This will bring the prospective person right before you and with a resume in hand if they have any initiative. People who just want to leave a number aren't worth it. If they can't make the effort to put something on paper, would you want them working around your expensive machinery and facing your customers? It's up to them to impress you and sell themselves from the very first impression

You can quickly look at the candidate's appearance, how they interact with you, and if you haven't got time to talk right then you can make an appointment to come back later. Be wary if they come in at lunchtime when you're busy – it suggests they don't know much about the industry.

Chances are that if they walk in the door and hand you a resume they live locally or are intending to move to the area. This helps with getting to work on time and may be useful when you need staff at short notice. It also shows they have the motivation to get out there and sell themselves.

### Newspapers

Advertising in papers is hit and miss. Probably more miss than hit these days. Unless you're looking for a chef, cook or barista in a salaried position, you'll probably end up talking to a lot of time wasters. If you use newspapers, look at local papers as they will attract people living locally.

### Internet and social media
This is inexpensive and efficient, as people can drop you an email and you can field enquiries later. This is a growing area to source people – just do a search and you'll find a number of suitable websites. If you have one, your website is a good place to advertise.

Social media is a huge source of potential staff. If you have a Facebook and/or Instagram page, put a message on there. You may find your next employee is an existing customer or someone already an advocate of your vision. LinkedIn is more focused on 'professional' positions; however, the network spreads far and wide and someone always knows someone looking for work.

### Job networks
Job networks work in conjunction with the government and attract funding to provide people with assistance and training to obtain employment. It's more than likely you'll get a visit from several different networks.

This is a double-edged sword. Most of the people these agencies try to place in the hospitality industry are returning to work after a long absence. They might be returning after having children or dealing with a personal issue. They might have been retrenched and be over skilled workers. They might have physical or mental health issues. They could be new immigrants or immigrants who have been working within their communities, both of whom may have language difficulties. There are also a fair number of people who don't wish to work and are just going through the motions.

To make it simple and put it bluntly, we will just say it – it's like looking for roses amongst the thorns. There may be a beautiful flower in there, but you need to be prepared to get scratched by a few thorns before you find that rose.

There is no doubt that most of these people are keen and want to work, but are they suitable for customer service? The notion that hospitality is an unskilled field is coming to an end, and employees are expected to multi-task: to do dishes, operate tills, clean, think on their feet and make excellent coffee. In one of the most competitive businesses in the world, you don't want to have people just standing around or creating a bad impression. These agencies provide a great service and can offer some benefits to your business, but you need to be open and patient.

# Subsidies

Subsidies may be available from employment agencies for people who have disabilities or have been out of work for long periods. Generally, the longer the period away from work, the higher the subsidy. The subsidy means being reimbursed for anywhere from 50 to 90 percent of the employee's wages for a specified time. The agency may also offer certain courses to assist the employees.

Employer beware! This arrangement can work out, and give you the opportunity to develop someone while your business gets some financial support. The question you have to ask is: how much effort will that take, and will this person be a hindrance or a help?

Sometimes it isn't worth upsetting the balance you have with current staff, especially if the subsidised employee requires a high level of supervision. If you think you almost need another person to help out, then it's a win-win situation. You can put on another person cheaply, and if you're lucky you will find the right person for the job just as it's being created. If not, at least they got some experience.

### Ben:

*I employed a lady via an employment agency. I took her on for food preparation: basic items such as focaccias and muffins. One day I walked in and saw a dozen fried eggs sitting behind the counter. I asked a staff member why there were fried eggs behind the counter, to which he shrugged and said, 'I don't know, Anna put them there'.*

*I found out that over the weekend she visited a café and had a bacon and egg focaccia. Having enjoyed it, she decided to add fried egg to every focaccia we prepared for the day: ham, cheese, tomato and fried egg; feta, olives, semi-dried tomato and fried egg; corned beef, cheese, hot English mustard…and yep…fried egg. The manager had spotted the reinvented focaccias and asked her to remake them, hence a dozen fried eggs just sitting there.*

*I explained to Anna that while it was great she was thinking of new things, she can't make changes without running them past someone else. Days later I walked into the kitchen to find Anna trying to get a piece of raisin toast out of the toaster with a knife… the toaster was still plugged in. I screamed at her to stop, which freaked us both out. It just hadn't occurred to me that she hadn't used toasters before as they were rarely used where she came from. These and other issues can arise due to cultural differences which are not anyone's fault but certainly are great opportunities to learn.*

# Potential Employees

### Parents returning to work
Parents returning to work can make great employees. Many have worked in all sorts of jobs but have been out of their fields too long to easily get back in. Others just want a part-time job to get out of the house and maybe some decent conversation. Generally, they are capable, hands-on, excellent with customers and reliable. The downside is that if the kids get sick they have to stay home, especially single parents with little support. Also, you may be getting slammed in the afternoon and need someone for that extra thirty minutes, but the kids need to be picked up.

### Students
University students are a great resource, and most of them need part time work. Most are great, but you also get your fair share of knowit-alls – after all, they might be doing a law degree! You need to watch for complacency with this group, as they have no intention of doing this for the rest of their lives.

Limitations with students can include inconvenient timetables and needing time off for exams. They also tend to ask for heaps of extra hours during the holidays then want to go away with friends at the last minute for a week at the beach. Students make great employees as long as you can work around their schedules.

### The overseas student
Foreign students are very keen to work and probably efficient in their country, but if there is a communication problem you'll spend more time explaining what you want than actually getting it done . Their language skills can be helpful, and they can be a pleasure to have around, but be prepared for a language barrier. Unless their English is excellent, of course.

### *Ben:*
*I had an employee who was very smart, but had a habit of questioning everything I said. Sometimes the simplest task was excruciating. I was on a call with the phone on my shoulder and asked, 'Could you please pass me the pen?' while pointing at a pen on the bench. She looked at me and went 'Aaaay?' 'Could you please pass me the pen', I repeated. She picked up the pen, looking at me again. 'Yes, could you please pass me the pen', I said. Still holding it up and looking at me she said 'You want me… to pass… you the pen?'*

*'Yes, can I please have the pen?' Slowly the pen was handed to me with an incredulous look of why the hell could you possibly want the pen.*

**Check their visas. Travellers on holidays may not be allowed to work and are taxed at a higher rate. Check online for tools you can use to check a candidate's work rights, including any limitations on hours and types of work.**

## Musicians

Just waiting for their big break. They might be very talented and work well, but these guys will want to play their own music when you're not around and have no idea that the customers don't wish to listen to obscure thrash metal while sipping their lattes. Make sure they have a washing machine as they have a propensity to throw the same clothes on from the gig the night before. Keep on top of that, and overall musicians are good to have around. If you have a venue that can hold gigs, harness their love of music and get them to run some gigs that suit your venue. Be nice, and when they get their break you'll probably be mentioned in a song!

## The alternative crowd

Positivity and patchouli fills the air. Beautiful souls who can be an asset when they're focused. The alternative crowd are a wonderful crew to have around as long as the dreadlocks are tied back and they wear shoes. They will want to make the menu organic, vegetarian and vegan and will want to recycle everything. However, they'll need time off for major alternative festivals, ranging from a day to a week. They will also put coffee grind out the back and forget it until it's time to tend the veggie patch. Taking the coffee grind home is great for the garden, but will stink up your space if not disposed of.

## The budding entrepreneur

Awesome employees who are keen to learn, eager to make the place better, and keen to take on responsibility. After two weeks they'll want to tell you how to run your business – after all, they'll be running their own one day. The danger is they might want to tell other staff, and you, how to do your jobs and upset the team culture and morale. This usually happens after about three to six months.

## Trainees

Depending on the size and operation of your place, you may be able to employ a trainee who can work most of the week and do one day at school or TAFE. Explore this with local hospitality educators and you may find a young employee wanting to learn. If you have a qualified chef you might be able to offer apprenticeships that attract government incentives.

**Work experience placements**

In Australia, as part of high school education students complete a week or two of practical work experience in their chosen field. You may at some point be asked to give a young person work experience. Honestly, unless you have many little jobs for them to do, they can get in the way. They need to be supervised closely if they lack confidence or initiative, which is common. You will be required to give your student a nominal daily fee, but it is very cheap and you can give them a bit more if you wish.

*Ben:*

*Having said that, I have found a few* students *who were keen and good operators. (I had my girlfriend's daughter hanging around one day and she started clearing tables. If it wasn't illegal to employ a ten-year-old I would have – she showed more initiative than some of my adult staff!)*

# Interviewing and hiring

If interviewing staff is a new experience for you, you might want to use some of the following pointers - and if you know anyone experienced at interviewing staff, by all means ask them for some advice. Building the right team around you is critical for success. They will be representing your business and reflecting your brand.

So let's get started. You have Mary, a prospective employee, in front of you, and in the first few seconds you'll have an opinion. This is a natural instinct when meeting anyone for the first time. If your gut is screaming 'No!' now or at any other time, it's worth listening to it, as it can turn out to be right. First impressions: How is Mary dressed? Is her attire appropriate for your venue? Does she appear confident? Does she smile and seem relaxed? Does she maintain eye contact? How does she communicate?

**Experience**

Check her resume to see where she has worked, and the frequency of job changes. Is Mary currently working? Why is she leaving? If she's not working, why did she leave her last employer?

**Interests**

What does Mary think is important and what can she bring to your business? Why does she want to work at your café? What hobbies and personal interests does she have?

### Availability
What hours does she want? Is she prepared and available to work nights, weekends and emergency shifts? What other commitments does she have? Ask about family commitments, study or interests that may affect her ability to work.

### References
It's up to you whether you wish to check references. It's not generally a common practice in this industry, but can save you potential issues down the track with a simple phone call. If you are looking at filling a manager position, we recommend making a few enquiries.

### Pay
What hourly rate does she want? It's important to ask to ensure the person is in line with your budget and pay expectations.

After the first few minutes you will have decided whether you're interested in going further. If you don't think you'll give the candidate a shot, cut it short and stop wasting time. Maybe suggest they try another place you know of, to show goodwill. If you don't feel comfortable telling the person you don't think they're suitable, tell them that you will call within twenty-four hours if you would like them to come in for a trial. It's far better to tell them straight away if possible, so they don't get their hopes up.

If considering employing a candidate, get them to come in for a trial to see if they can do what they claim. A person claiming to be a barista should be able to make an excellent coffee on the spot on any machine with any type of beans. The trial also gives them a chance to see if they like your place, and your staff an opportunity to see what they think of the new starter.

If the trial goes well, sit with them afterwards and explain exactly what's next and your expectations.

# Ground rules
Keep these key points in mind as the basis of your employer/employee relationship.

1) If they simply do their job and do as you ask, they get paid. The more they help you achieve what you want, the more they get what they want – money!

2) You employ them to make your life easier. If they don't you have no need for them in a working capacity.

Be sure to explain when pays are due and have them complete relevant forms and paperwork. Paperwork should outline their rate of pay and other conditions, such as probation and termination. Ideally, provide staff with their rosters in advance so they know to be available for their working shifts.

You can find templates for employee paperwork at www.thecafeguys.com.au.

### Ben:

*I once interviewed a lady who looked me in the eye and told me she was a barista. As we were busy I couldn't get her to show me her skills so I asked her to describe the process of how she would make a coffee. This was her exact answer. 'First I'd boil the kettle… then add coffee'. I was silent and stared at her, urging her to tell me more. I just wanted to see if she added milk. I then asked her, 'You don't know anything about coffee do you?' As she answered honestly, and I thought at least she admitted it with a smile, I decided to give her a try. Two weeks later I had to let her go. Although she was a fantastic girl, she just wasn't suited to hospitality. She found her vocation soon after and remained a customer for some time.*

**If you are new to hospitality try to employ staff you can learn from. They will know more than you could ever study on the subject and can give you ideas from their previous experience to help run efficiently.**

# Pay conditions

Pay and other entitlements vary from country to country and state to state. Understand what the minimum wages, conditions, and entitlements are where you're from. You may get employees asking for cash to avoid tax or to not impact their earnings through other benefits they may be receiving. Depending on where you're from, this may be illegal so ensure you understand if there is a risk involved for you and your business.

### Ben:

*My motto when employing was a version of a saying you might have heard: you meet everyone for a reason, a season or a lifetime. My version is a reason, a season but never a lifetime. I know that my employees will move on for one reason or another. I say to the new staff, 'I will help you get what you want if you will help me get what I want – an honest, reliable, punctual and competent employee'. I have been blessed in that I have always had, reliable staff.*

### Petar:

*I came from a background of 10 years in Human Resources and Recruiting so having a process in place was important to me. The people you hire in your business can make or break it. They represent the brand so for me it was important to be more thorough than what is considered standard for the industry. In addition to this, I wanted to get into business to create a working life I would love. If I was going to spend alot of my time (especially in the beginning) in the business, I wanted to make sure it was with people I was going to enjoy spending time with and be able to create an enjoyable atmosphere to work and build relationships in. This reflects back to customers as well.*

*When hiring an employee, I spent quite alot of time finding what I felt was the right person for a position. This included keeping in mind other personalities (as well as my own) and how they would fit within that dynamic. Getting the wrong person can at best waste time, money and energy in needing to oversee everything they do, and at worst it can cost you money, damage customer and supplier relationships and ruin the reputation of your business.*

*You can find the Recruitment Process I followed at www.thecafeguys.com.au, including effective interview and reference checking questions.*

THE CAFE GUYS

# PART 3
# READY TO START?

# CHAPTER 13
# YOUR CAFÉ & YOUR CLIENTELE

Y ou've made it. Your premises is set up, the menu is written, all stock has been ordered and staff are ready to start. Now all you need are customers.

## Time to launch

We'll talk in detail about marketing later, but if you want someone other than your mum and your best friend to walk through the door on the first day, it might be an idea to organise a special event to kick-start your new business.

It doesn't have to be anything fancy. Offer an opening special or two-for-one deal to anyone who walks in on the first day or even week. Perhaps you could contact local business owners and ask them to stop by. If you have time, a letterbox drop in the local area advising neighbours that there's a new café opening up might just get things off to a good start. If you put up a few streamers or hang a bunch of balloons outside you're bound to attract at least a few curious passersby.

At the very least, invite all of your family and friends to come and toast your new venture. Maybe bake a special cake and open a few bottles of champagne.

Of course, depending on the nature of your business, you might even want to go all fancy with an after-dark cocktail party and 100 guests. It doesn't matter what you do, just mark the day somehow, and try to create a bit of a party atmosphere.

## What motivates customers to come to you?

You'll have customers coming through your doors from day one however this is no time to start taking things for granted. If you want them to stay loyal,

72

you've got to keep them happy and give them a reason to come back. You need a combination of the following:

• Superior products – they like what you provide.
• Good service and friendly staff – they feel comfortable and happy at your place.
• A great vibe – they enjoy the space.
• Convenience – you're nearby and easy to get to.
• Point of difference - you offer different products to nearby cafés

You should strive for all of these things. The more boxes you tick the better. While ticking all the boxes is important, probably the most important thing you can do to keep them coming back is to be consistent.

## Be true to your vision and strategy

Getting your mix right is paramount, but working out which of these is your signature, the essence of your café, that helps you be consistent, focused and maintain your vision.

If 'quick and easy' is your mantra, then fast service implemented through a limited product range is going to be your minimum standard. In this instance, the more complexity you add, with a larger range menu or trying to get more sophisticated with how you present your food, will only impact your original strategy. That may result in you losing the loyal customers you had gained by being fast.

If quality and style is your key aim, then it is imperative you don't start chasing sales by dropping your prices and lowering your quality to go after the 'quick and easy' customers.

Cafés that have a strong vision and statement about the sort of product, service, vibe and convenience they are offering their customers from the beginning, who stay true to this vision, (hopefully improving along the way) give customers confidence in knowing they can come back for what they are looking for and reliably get it.

A faithful bunch of regular customers are far more valuable to you than the ones just looking for the latest fad. You know that those customers will be quick to go when something new or different turns up. You will need to work out if the investment you put into getting those customers (updating décor, changing the menu, changing prices, etc.) will be worth the return you get from your new clients? Will you be able to convert them into regular customers? And will your current customers stay loyal?

Look around at the cafés doing well and you will see consistency across most or all of these things (product, service, vibe and convenience), and you will also see a theme they are loyal to.

What if you get bored of your café style? Consider long and hard before reinventing yourself to something totally new. Evolution is easier than revolution!

Consider all your options including selling your existing business and acquiring a new one closer to your new vision. Closing up shop and magically becoming something different takes time, money and experience. As you get more experienced you may be up for that sort of challenge, but beware of the costs and risk you are incurring as a result of your boredom or thinking 'the grass is greener' with someone else's strategy or passion.

**Create a simple survey and ask your customers what they like. Use an online survey site such as Survey Monkey, which allows you to send a survey out to your Facebook friends, email contacts and post a link on your website (www.surveymonkey.com). Offer an incentive to encourage people to participate - e.g. A free coffee for each completed survey. or a $50 voucher for one lucky participant.**

# Consistency

Have you ever gone to the same café and had a coffee that's different from how you experienced it the time before? You cannot afford to be inconsistent as you will lose customers very quickly. Your coffee, tea, mocha or hot chocolate must be the same every time unless a customer asks for something different. Consistency is key - not just in coffee, but in everything you do.

Each time a customer returns they should be offered exactly the same service, atmosphere, meal or coffee they had last time. The quality of the produce, recipes, temperature of dishes, texture, presentation and even the plates you use must be the same every time. The hours of operation, music, lighting, the whole experience, must always be the same.

**Ben:**
*My business evolved over time. Customers were never guaranteed that the tables would be in the same spot, or they would sit on the same chair, but this inconsistency was consistent and*

*part of the charm of my place. I got away with it because it made my place quirky. However, my food and coffee was as consistent as I could make it. Consistency is key!*

### Petar:
*We made changes through the years in our business, however it was always to facilitate growth and evolve without reinventing ourselves. We would upgrade tables, chairs and decor to freshen up the atmosphere - make things new and exciting for our regular clientele and continue to attract visitors and have people discovering and talking about us. We would also change and update the menu, but items would always be consistent with our vision and what we were known for - healthy, fresh, high quality options served with consistency.*

# The little things

We are in the hospitality game, which means being hospitable. It means acknowledging people and being grateful for their business. It's crucial that you acknowledge your customers when they enter and when they leave. You should certainly say 'hi' or at least give them a nod if you're busy serving someone else. Give regulars a nod or a wink. There is nothing worse than going into a place for the first time and not being acknowledged or getting a lacklustre greeting.

Smiles win customers. First impressions count so make a good one and increase your chance of repeat business.

Cleanliness is a big issue, but there are a few things that contribute to the appearance of cleanliness that you need to stay on top of. Make sure tables are wiped as soon as they're cleared. If you're busy and there are dishes on the table, at least people can see you are busy and haven't got to clearing the table, however, if tables are cleared but not wiped it just makes your venue look dirty.

### Ben:
*Barry is one of our regulars, and although he has a few watering holes, he comes in early almost daily for a quiet ale, goes off to*
*do his rounds, and usually comes back in the afternoon. He sits quietly and happily has a chat if you talk to him, but, for the most part sits and enjoys his beer. I noticed one day that Barry, who appreciates the little things, didn't have a coaster under his beer and was sitting with a puddle of condensation in front of him. I promptly went over to wipe the table and give him a coaster. Good old Barry should never be taken for granted. Let's do the sums: if he buys two pots of beer daily that's nine dollars, and he does this 340 days of the year. He's spending a minimum of $3,060 at the bar in a year! What type of customer is he? A bloody good one and he deserves our attention. Make sure your staff understand that people like Barry pay their wages.*

**Petar:**

*Similarly to Ben, I had quite a few customers who would come in for a quiet cup of coffee and a chat daily. While in a single day it's only $3.50, over the course of a year adds up to over $1,000. But it's even more than that - because they feel welcomed and we make them feel special, if they ever want somewhere to bring friends and family for breakfast or others ask them about a good local cafe, we're the ones who are top of their list. Suddenly someone they've recommended us to comes in for regular breakfasts, and also continues the cycle of recommendations provided we maintain our level of service. Never underestimate the power of a single customer!*

**Take good care of regulars, one coffee or beer five times a week adds up.**

# The ABCD scale – the customer is not always right

Not every customer will be as delightful as Barry and you need to understand there are different types. Customers fall into one of four grades, and although you should be courteous to all customers, there are some you will want to spend more time and effort on.

**A customers** are regular, friendly and happy. They enjoy your business, respect your time, and spend more than your average client. They only make legitimate complaints and are often apologetic when they do so. You should know their name and how they prefer their coffee.

**B customers** are regular but don't come in for interaction; they just want to grab their order and get on their way. They'll extend pleasantries, grab their coffee for the day and are off.

**C customers** are irregular and don't spend that much. They don't wish to interact, and can be somewhat unfriendly, almost to the point of rudeness. They can also be people who need or want attention and make odd requests to get it.

**D customers** are painful. They complain, make unusual requests to get your attention, think that nothing is ever right, and tell you how bad your coffee was last time but are back again anyway. They ask for credit, aren't forthcoming with payment, or act as though you owe them something.

The bottom line is you want your business to be made up mostly of A and B customers and tolerate C customers as necessary. Refuse the odd requests and hankerings of D and C customers, and tell them simply that you do not extend credit or can't adapt the menu a certain way if it's not practical or convenient for you. They will either become better customers or they'll no longer come in, which means you can focus on your better customers.

# Complaints

As sure as the sun rises in the east and sets in the west, you will eventually be dealing with complaints at some point. It's very important not to take them personally, as hard as that will be, especially when you're starting out and likely to make mistakes. As time goes by, you'll get better at dealing with complaints.

When somebody complains, listen to what the issue is and do your best to rectify it immediately if possible. A coffee that's too hot or too cold is an easy fix; remake it straight away. Meals can be a different matter and may require a discount or free meal to rectify the situation… especially if an A or B customer makes the complaint.

Many complaints can be avoided by making sure glassware and cutlery are clean, and staff know exactly what they're doing. Make a point of being vigilant about your products, their quality and presentation. If you noticed a latte go out with less than a centimeter of froth, consider calling it back. If your staff do exactly what you want and you know it, you can back them 100% when a complaint comes in. You may even find that the complaint is more of a customer preference that wasn't made clear when they placed their order.

### Ben:
*I had a regular customer who would send one of her employees to buy the morning coffees. Her business was in a small complex that had three coffee shops, but she chose to send her staff for a 20 minute return trip to my place five days a week. I found her to be rather rude and negative when she came in herself.*

*Sure enough, one day she complained about the coffee. The staff member who served her, who I trusted to make the coffee properly, came out the back to fill me in. The customer had been offered another and refused. She was then offered a refund, which she also refused. I was told she wanted to talk to me. I put aside what I was doing and walked out to ask what the problem was. 'The coffee was disgusting!' I was told. I again offered to make her another coffee or give her a refund, and once again she refused both. I then said, 'If you don't want any more coffees and you don't want your money back, what would you like?' She just shook her head and said, 'I just, I just, I just want to complain.' I said her complaint was noted.*

*Sometimes you just can't win, but in this case it all made sense later when I found out that her marriage was breaking down and she needed to let off steam. The very next day she was back in buying coffee. Disgusting hey?*

**Petar:**

*Reasonable complains should be very willingly accepted. They're potentially an opportunity for you to improve on or address certain aspects of your business, giving you customer insight to review what occurred and why. In most cases they're easily resolved and usually due to human error. If it's something more serious, make sure you investigate thoroughly to ensure it doesn't happen again and update your processes and inform staff accordingly.*

*In the social media age, everyone's a critic. We had a few negative reviews, (only around 3 or so in our entire tenure, thankfully!) two were reasonable, and one was less justified. Reviews on Facebook and other platforms are visible to all members of the public and allow you the opportunity to reply. Take advantage of this to turn the situation in your favour for anyone viewing your customer feedback. The two reasonable reviews were due to key ingredients being left out, and as a result those customers posted negative feedback on our page. I posted a response accordingly and offered to rectify the situation. Both times this was graciously accepted and one even changed the negative review to a positive due to the way I handled it. Even with the unreasonable review (customer missed the sign at the entrance - and on the menu - instructing customers to order at the counter, and she waited at her table for service which never came), I responded apologising for the misunderstanding that occurred and that we will seek to improve sign visibility and clarity of the instruction. The worst thing you can do is lash out or hit back, as tempting as it may be, especially if you feel it was unreasonably harsh. Keep your cool and respond in a way you would want to be responded to if you had complained.*

*Regardless of the negative reviews, people who view the feedback will see an owner who cares about their business and respects any and all of their customers, seeking to limit any concerns and listen and seek to address any issues. Public perception will still be in your favour. As well as the negative reviews, good practice would be to acknowledge and thank the positive reviews as well!*

# CHAPTER 14
# STAFF AND LEADERSHIP

Customers aren't just the people who eat your food and drink your beer. You also have internal customers – your staff. One of the best ways to keep your regular customers happy is to make sure your employees are doing their jobs as well, and are happy in their roles.

## Staff issues

As an employer of staff, you're now responsible for managing other people and their problems. If you haven't been a manager or leader before, you're in for a treat. We all have issues and at some point you'll have problems with your staff.

People lose sight of the fact that we're in the hospitality game. The word says it all – it's our job to be hospitable no matter what is going on in our private lives, and sometimes it requires a bit of acting on our behalf. Guess what though? We are human, and some of us aren't good at the acting part of the job. Be considerate and empathetic to staff regarding their problems, but be clear about your priorities as a business owner. Set clear expectations about roles and responsibilities. If a staff member's issues prevent them from fulfilling their duties, they shouldn't be there.

Now let's look at some of those issues.

***Ben:***
*Sometimes I would come to work with a frown on my face without realising and would worry my employees, who thought I was mad until someone finally spoke to me about it pulled me up on it and discovered I was stressed about a bill or something. I hadn't realised I was letting it show on my face!*

## Stealing

There's a belief that if you have a cash business someone will be stealing. Sometimes staff see money come in and think you must be making a killing. If they see themselves as the reason for making your fortune, they may feel justified to take a little. Install cameras, track your takings, manage your stock and watch for awkwardness in staff when you're around. If you're adamant someone is stealing, get proof and catch them out, or if you think it's a big loss, consider getting a professional investigator in. The Australian Tax Office allows you to write off an amount as loss, but you need to consult your accountant on how to claim this.

In the end, however, you can only hope to minimise losses. Overall if you are treating staff well, you should be able to trust them to do the right thing. You would rather think of them as honest than waste energy worrying if they're not. See Chapter 16 about scams and rip-offs for more information on stealing and deception.

## Punctuality

Why can't people be on time? Good practice would be for staff to be on the premises ten minutes early so they can put their things away, have a coffee and be ready to work at the designated start time. Being late occasionally is okay, it happens for all sorts of reasons, but be wary about serial offenders whose excuses include:

• I slept through my alarm
• I'm sick (in which case don't come in)
• I had a flat tyre
• The traffic was bad
• The tram, train or bus was late
• The dog got out
• I thought I started at…
• It was raining so hard I couldn't leave the house, I didn't have an umbrella

In the era of mobile phones, staff should be able to let you know if they'll be late well in advance.

Shifts are timed to cater for busy times. You need staff to be prepping for business or serving customers. If there's a staff changeover and you have one person waiting to finish you can't be left wondering if their replacement is going to show.

Texting has become the preferred way to communicate and can be useful for quick communication but shouldn't replace calls or used to avoid uncomfortable discussions regarding why they aren't at work.

*I learned a valuable lesson from one of my managers. He would rather work one staff member down, or even alone, than have staff arrive late for a shift. I walked in one day and he was on his own, with two staff members down. When I asked where everyone was he told me they had both been late, and he'd told them to come back tomorrow when they could be on time. I still admire the man for that.*

*Being late regularly shows a lack of respect for you, your business and your customers. Don't tolerate it.*

# Laziness

A lazy employee lacks motivation. Unfortunately you'll attract staff who are only there for the money, and that's fine, but are you getting what you want? Are you getting value for your money? Try to find ways to motivate them.

Beware of employees who feel they're owed something just for showing up. At the first sign of this, sit down for a conversation or dismiss them. Your business cannot afford to have staff that aren't pleasant and attentive. They won't care about their job, which means they don't care about you, your team or your business either.

Laziness includes being lazy-minded. Make lists of tasks with detailed instructions for those who refuse to engage common sense. This can be useful because the lists become a working manual that can be given to new employees.

You may have regular employees who have preferences for certain jobs. For instance, some people love cleaning, others prefer organising cutlery, and others like arranging displays or shelves. You may be able to designate preferred jobs to staff members permanently. That's fine as long as everything gets done, and everybody knows how to do the job if the regular person isn't there.

# Personal hygiene

Poor personal hygiene and hospitality do not mix. Nobody wants to smell body odour just as their meal or drink is delivered. From our experience, it has been young men who have needed to be reminded of the importance of personal hygiene. If this happens, quietly pull them aside and tactfully explain that you expect them to come to work in clean clothes and wearing deodorant. For those who tend to perspire more than normal, suggest bringing in a spare shirt, and also keep deodorant on the premises for emergencies. If you're hiring people who are more natural in their use of self-care products, remember there are many natural solutions that can be used.

**Ben:**

*I had one staff member who was great in every way, but he smelt bad. I discussed how to broach the subject with my manager, and decided to go straight up to him and say, 'Mate, sorry to say this but something around you smells. You sort of smell old or something.' He looked at me and said, 'Yeah sorry, I didn't get to shower before work.' The next night the same thing happened, but he said he had just had a shower. We finally discovered that he liked shopping at a secondhand store, and would often buy something and wear it to work without washing it.*

You can see what a delicate matter it is to tell someone they smell, but you have to be up front and ask as politely as possible.

# Drugs and alcohol

Drugs and alcohol are a problem for your business if staff performance is affected.

You will notice staff dropping the ball occasionally; however when it happens frequently you need to start asking questions.

**Ben:**

*One of my best employee's pastimes was to smoke cannabis. What she did out of hours was none of my business, but occasionally she'd be a bit forgetful at work. When she stopped smoking dope (funny how it's called dope, hey?) she was as sharp as a knife; an awesome employee.*

*After 12 months things began to slide again and I asked, 'I'm starting to notice you're making a lot of mistakes and I was wondering if you're smoking again?' She admitted that she was, and I asked if she didn't mind telling me how much. It turns out she regularly smoked before coming to work every day. I told her what she did on her own time is her own business, but she just can't come to work like that.*

*She quit abruptly two weeks later. You can't stop it or control it, but you need to be mindful that it exists and can affect your business. I have used an illicit drug as an example but since writing this chapter I have had to dismiss two people due to being at work intoxicated. One was a male, and one was a female, both seemingly intelligent adults. Drugs or alcohol, it's a dangerous environment regardless.*

**Petar:**

*Drugs and employees have never been a problem for my business, however I have had conversations with employees regarding their alcohol consumption. They haven't necessarily come to work drunk, but regularly went out to drink after work and occasionally wouldn't be in a condition to work their shift the next day. I had a conversation around this and the situation improved. While what people do in their own time is their business, if it impacts their ability to perform what is expected of them it becomes your business. Talk to your staff so they understand your expectations and repercussions if their behaviour and disregard for your business continues. Be respectful and clear with your communication and you will arrive at the right outcome.*

# Texting

With the introduction of texting and social media the productivity in many cafés and bars has declined. It seems to be the way many people communicate these days, but there is no place for it in your workplace. Ban phones unless it's an emergency. It looks bad from a business perspective, and staff shouldn't be doing it when there's work to do.

Even if it's quiet, they need to find something to do other than texting friends. They can do it on their breaks.

### Ben:

*I had one employee so focussed on his text conversation that he wasn't attentive. I was sitting there in plain sight having drinks with friends. We had been sitting on empty glasses for at least 15 minutes and it was quiet. I would have expected him to come and offer us another one or at least take our glasses. In the end I sent him a text asking for another drink, which he found hilarious. Probably wouldn't have found it as hilarious if he realised it was one of the reasons he was replaced.*

# Be a leader

As a leader you need to demonstrate the right attitude for your staff to follow. You are in a service industry, so you need to inspire your team and motivate them. You should help facilitate their growth and guide staff who wish to learn. You need to set the standard and be a role model of what you expect from your staff. So be sure to greet customers, be neat and presentable in your appearance and set the benchmark of how you would want everyone else in the business to conduct themselves in all areas. If staff see you ignore customers, walk past rubbish on the floor or texting while its busy, it sends the wrong message to your staff.

The performance of your business will be a direct reflection of you. Who do you need to be in order to achieve your vision? To attract customers? To attract and retain the right calibre of staff? To lead a successful business? E.g. Do you need to be more confident? Assertive? Organised? Approachable?

Ask yourself who you are being right now. If it isn't consistent with who you know you need to be, you've found some gaps to address. This is where a good coach or mentor can come in and support you.

A lot of staff issues can be avoided by demonstrating strong leadership and good interview techniques that ensure you hire the right people in the first place. Once you have your team, help your staff to understand and share your vision for the café. Ideally, try to find staff that are motivated by being a part of building something, and take pride in helping to make the business successful.

Your staff need to know where you stand in the business. They need to feel secure. Make decisions quickly, especially those that affect your staff, but make informed changes. If it takes time to make a decision and you can't give an answer about an issue to your staff, explain why you're taking your time and involve them in your decision-making.

Stand up for your team as long as you can do it with integrity and you know they have done the right thing. Try not to belittle or talk down to them in public or in front of other staff members. If there is a delicate issue to bring up, do it in private. When you make a mistake, admit it. Being the boss is not an excuse to pretend you're right all the time.

As you grow so does your business, commit to getting better at everything you do and encourage staff to do the same. Wine and coffee companies offer on-site training but also explore what other courses are available. This will demonstrate that you're interested in your staff. Any time you get freebies or samples from suppliers share them with employees and get their feedback. Take them to trade shows if time permits and sample new products together. See Chapter 19 - Training.

### Ben:
*One of my best employees had a self-limiting belief that she would never amount to anything. She was a single mum who was scared of getting things wrong, believed she was incapable of making decisions, and believed she couldn't earn over $500 a week. We played a little game where she would ask me about a problem, and I would just stare at her. She would run through one solution after another, and then decide what to do without a word from me. I believed in her and as a result she blossomed, breaking a number of self-defeating patterns and becoming an excellent and reliable employee for years.*

# Create a culture

Culture can simply be stated as the 'how we do things around here'. It will be the mantra that your café needs to live and breathe by. As the leader you will set the standard for this, so remember your actions will be closely watched and followed by your staff. For example, Ben is affectionately called the 'Coffee Nazi' by his team. This is a clear example of the sort of culture that he has set around the level of service and standard of product that is served to his customers. Culture is often defined by the 'unwritten rules' but can be even more powerful when you make these 'unwritten rules' very visible and reinforce them to your staff.

Culture is what will make your café very different from the one down the road. It can add untold value to the product and services you offer. It will be what helps you attract and retain the right staff. If you value timeliness, quality and efficiency, then you will need to reinforce these things to your staff members during every shift. By calling them when they don't get it right, or even more importantly, by recognising and praising them when they do get it right, you are setting the tone for what is expected from everyone. These are the non-negotiables you value.

Culture is what will make your café's vision authentic and real for your customers. If you are going for a health-café like Petar did, then your culture needs to include vibrant and positive staff, healthy menu items and an abundance of respect for anything associated with exercise, health and wellbeing. Being true to your culture requires you to be brave and have tough conversations about even the most minor deviations from it.

*Petar:*
*There was an incident where one of my staff members were eating a chocolate bar behind the counter. While they were trying to keep it hidden from view, it was still visible to customers and myself. I took them aside in private and addressed the issue with them - firstly because they were eating outside their designated break time and when they were supposed to be working and serving customers. Secondly because they were sending the wrong message and being inconsistent with our brand. While there is nothing wrong with chocolate in moderation, it's not what our business stood for and not why customers came to us. People can go anywhere for chocolate, they come to us because we stay away from refined and processed items. The staff member understood and apologised and there was no further issue. Stay loyal to your culture and your brand, and your customers and staff will too.*

# Termination

Sometimes you just have to let someone go. To save time and energy on a dispute, check your rights and the rights of employees. This is relatively straightforward, so know where you stand and remember it's your business and your livelihood. You pay employees for a service, if they don't or can't provide it you should replace them as soon as practicable.

If the employee is quite new or commits gross misconduct such as stealing, you may not need to give notice. In this case, terminate the contract as soon as possible. Do not keep them on until you find a replacement. A disgruntled or unsuitable employee can damage your business through bad service, by telling customers they're leaving, or even by making up stories about you or your café.

If a longer serving employee is no longer meeting the required standard, have a conversation with them and give them the opportunity to improve. Be clear in your expectations and next steps and give them the best possible chance to succeed in your business. If there is no change within a set timeframe, it's in your best interest to let them go. Don't keep them just because they used to be a good employee.

Check appropriate legislation and be sure you're following the right process legally.

# CHAPTER 15

# LEGALITIES

For many of you this will be the annoying part of running a business. Unfortunately it's also a critical part. Getting into legal trouble will be the quickest way to go bankrupt or get your business closed down. So take the time to understand these potential issues and make sure all your legal bases are covered.

## Occupational health and safety

As a business owner you have an obligation to your staff to provide a safe work environment and safe work practices. Large organisations have OH&S representatives and formal procedures to follow; for small business owners the liability remains the same but it's up to you to implement. You need to identify potential hazards and put in place practices that minimise the risk to you and your staff. Laminated information sheets and warnings are good to have on display.

Here are some real-life scenarios that we have seen in our businesses. Thankfully they were all minor, but any of them could have become a disaster:

• Using a knife to get toast out of a toaster that was still plugged in
• Cutting a finger on broken glass thrown into a bag rather than recycling
• Falling off an incorrectly positioned ladder (that was Ben; luckily he landed on his feet)
• Burning through the cord of a milkshake maker that was touching a sandwich press
• Minor burns from oven and coffee machine steam
• Minor burn from adding wet items to the fryer
• Cuts from glass breakage
• An employee who weighed well over 100kg standing full height on a stool to adjust a stereo rather than using the ladder that was five metres away
• Lifting strains

- Hitting heads on various items
- Finger jams in fridge
- Trips as a result of running
- Slip as a result of a spill not being cleaned

In Australia we live in a litigious society and it's best to focus on prevention, so we have made a short list of some areas to consider. This is not a complete guide, just something to get you thinking along the right lines.

## Cuts

Make sure knives are sharp and that staff know how to use them correctly. A blunt knife can be more dangerous than a sharp one. Correct cutting techniques should be taught to staff.

## Trips and slips

There will be lots of water, oils, cleaning fluids, and drink spillages that can cause a slip or fall. Use appropriate signage when cleaning and mopping. Mats used by staff to reduce the impact of standing on a hard floor all day can also cause a trip hazard.

## Running

When they're under pressure staff will run. It is crucial that they don't. The time saved by running to get something is never worth the injury caused by a fall or collision. A dropped plate or coffee will take fifteen minutes to clean up and will annoy your customers. Slow and steady wins the race every time.

## Falls

Staff can fall from stairs, chairs and ladders, including low step ladders. Staff should only use step ladders rather than chairs to reach for some items.

## Lifting

Depending on your venue, there can be anything from 50 kilogram kegs of beer, numerous boxes of drinks, bags of dry goods such a flour and other heavy products. Make sure staff know and use correct techniques for lifting and handling heavy items.

## Fire and burns

Make sure you have fire blankets and the appropriate fire extinguishers. Your local authorities will likely be checking these, but also beware that certain extinguishers are designed for different types of fires. For example, a foam extinguisher should be used on electrical and oil fires. Water sprayed into hot oil will cause an explosion as the oil reacts with water. Frying goods from frozen is an example of how this can happen – if there is any ice residue it will cause hot oil to react.

Also beware of chemical burns caused by cleaning products. Chemicals should come with Safety Data Sheets (SDS) that explain the properties of the chemical, how to store them and what to do in an emergency. Ask your suppliers for these.

## Electrical hazards

Make sure all wiring is in good condition, all power cords are protected from heat and from being severed. All wiring on utensils should be checked for stress. Most appliances in Australia have good safety ratings however it is worth getting a qualified test & tag inspector to check all your appliances regularly.

## Hazardous chemicals

Any cleaning chemicals are to be labelled and stored in a designated safe place. Safety data sheets as mentioned above are available on the internet, and a copy should be provided the first time you purchase these types of chemicals from a supplier. If you don't get one, ask!

## First aid kit

Keep a first aid kit on the premises, charts for resuscitation and a first aid manual. It sounds over the top, but what would happen if you or a staff member were to have an accident? Does the team know what to do? Make sure the first aid kit is up to date and has a few non-standard items like medically approved burn creams (for minor burns) and blue band aids for minor cuts. Keep the kit accessible and make sure all staff know where it is kept.

## Medical conditions

Staff should let you know of any pre-existing conditions they have, such as allergies or anything that may require first aid or it affects their duties. You should ask about this at the interview stage. A person with extreme allergies to peanuts is most likely in the wrong industry.

## Fatigue/stress management

Staff should manage their fatigue, but if you see a staff member under stress or tired, it's best that they rest. Sometimes you have a staff member who either wants to help or needs the money and will push themselves beyond a safe limit. Mistakes often happen when we're tired, and you might have to put a stop to this practice.

# Drug and alcohol usage

No drinking or drug use during or before a shift would be ideal. It's dangerous to you, your staff and the individual. This is hard to enforce with regards to drinking especially if you are a licensed venue and there is no real policy on it other than what you enforce.

*Ben:*
*I don't mind if my staff have a drink on a break as long as they are not affected when behind the bar.*

It's normal to provide a drink after a shift but limit these. If staff leave after being plied with alcohol and something happens to them on their way home, you may be held responsible.

# Tips for making health and safety important for all your staff.

• Create your list of health and safety expectations: All employees must read these expectations when they join the team. Give them a quiz to prove they have read it, if they fail the quiz; make them do it again until they pass before they commence working in your business. Creating clear expectations from the outset is important in managing your responsibilities and potential liabilities as an employer.

• Talk about and document incidents and near misses: Don't let an awkward conversation or the stress of a near miss let you lose an excellent opportunity to coach your staff in what could have been a better course of action to take. Thinking through incidents to prevent future accidents is vital and helps to protect you as an employer.

• Where possible, organise accredited training for staff. The reality is that small businesses have a harder time finding and making time to train staff even though the liability remains the same. Keeping the workplace safe is also the responsibility of each staff member. Nobody can afford to be complacent or rely on others to look out for them. Take initiative to provide a way to report and remedy incidents and hazards.

# Public liability

The health and safety of your staff is one issue, but you must also consider the health and safety of customers and other members of the public. You have a duty of care to your customers and anybody else who walks through your door.

Many of the issues discussed above will affect members of the public, and there are further issues that you need to consider.

# Food handling

Food handling skills can be a major problem. Food handling training isn't mandatory but adhering to safe practices are, and you must have a food safety supervisor in Australia. It is in everyone's interest to know how to handle food, clean and prepare it in a safe manner and environment. For their safety staff should know about food temperatures, handling of goods like fresh chicken, the importance of hygiene, and so forth. Staff could easily cause contamination if handling products incorrectly as well as putting customers at risk.

There are many courses both accredited and non-accredited as well as courses that are inexpensive or even free. Start with your state government website and visit your national website for training.

The number of times staff members sneeze, or wipe their noses or brow while preparing food without even being aware of it is incredible. Staff need to be aware that once they touch money or skin they need to wash
their hands before going back to food or coffee making. Don't be fooled that because they are wearing gloves it's cleaner as same rules apply, gloves must be changed too.

Fact sheets and templates for food safety practices should be available from your local authorities. These will include information on food handling, cross contamination, correct storage, reheating temperatures for food, personal hygiene and more. Get them and display them prominently.

Maintaining records is also a legal requirement in most countries. You need to label stock, record when it was opened and keep records on the storage of prepared foods, among other requirements.

A tip is to keep your dish and glass return, as well as your washing area separate from your preparation area.

**Ben:**
*A customer made a complaint that he found a piece of glass in a focaccia. This meant a mandatory inspection, despite my washing area being in another room from where the food was prepared. There was no proof of the glass being present, and not surprisingly we passed the inspection with flying colours.*

# Hygiene

Staff should start the day with clean clothes, clean body, hair tied back and minimal jewellery. They must wash their hands before touching food, and each time they leave a food preparation area then return to handling food. Either that or wear fresh gloves each time. Notice chefs don't wear gloves as they pose a threat to cutting as you lose sensitivity and latex melts when exposed to heat. I prefer clean hands every time.

I remember seeing a lady serve me wearing gloves at a takeaway outlet. She prepared my sandwich then, without taking the gloves off, took my money, gave me change and served the next person without changing gloves. Money is the dirtiest thing you will ever touch; the gloves are for customers' protection, not yours.

Your liability extends to the service of alcohol as well. Responsible Service of Alcohol is a compulsory course in Australia for any employee involved in the service of alcohol. Check with your state authority.

**Make staff aware of emergency procedures. Have an evacuation plan, medical emergency procedures, police and emergency numbers nearby. Keep fault and failure numbers for power, gas and water easily accessible.**

**Have a list of all contacts in case of emergency. Make sure staff know they can authorise a repair or at least have the right person for the job on their way out to your business.**

# Accounting and taxation

Unless you're knowledgeable about accounting, employ someone who is.

### Accountants

Get an accountant who knows about business-related tax and financial issues. It may be expensive to have an accountant do all your books, but if you start with a good one you can develop your relationship and he or she can get to know your business and give you tailored advice more efficiently and timely.

When choosing your accountant, feel free to question what they know about business and hospitality in particular – it's fair to find out their experience. Accountants with familiarity in the industry will be able to offer insight, advice and strategic direction in tandem with other advisors such as a coach to help you achieve your financial goals.

### Ben:
*My first accountant advised me to close down after my first year. I appreciated his honesty, but sixteen years later I'm still here! I was with my second accountant for ten years, and he handled all sorts of issues, but I only had him go over my end-of-year tax and my personal tax return. By that time I had the money side of my business under control.*

### Bookkeepers
Bookkeepers are a cheaper option than accountants, but even if you use a bookkeeper for your everyday accounting, you will still need to submit your paperwork to your accountant at the end of the financial year.

It's worthwhile getting a bookkeeper on board early to at least set you up, especially if you're planning to do your own books and have absolutely no idea about accounts and no interest in the subject. Be diligent and get an accounting program. The Australian Tax Office now offers a package you can use, but you can't go wrong using any mainstream package. If you're working with a bookkeeper or accountant, ask their advice on what to use, including to cloud based accounting such as Xero.

### Business activity statement (BAS)
In Australia you need to register to pay GST (Goods and Services Tax) once you turn over more than $75,000 a year. This means that you will have to start preparing quarterly BAS statements.

Here is what's really frustrating about paying BAS in the food industry. The majority of products you buy for your business will be GST free as they're primary produce – meat, bread, milk, coffee, vegetables and most food items. You turn all this into a beautiful dish, and you collect GST on everything you sell, except for a few items about which your bookkeeper or accountant will advise you. About 90 per cent of your product will attract GST.

### What does this mean?
It means that if all is going well and you're still in business, you not only have to pay the PAYG tax you collect for staff wages, but also the GST you collected less what you paid. You will be paying the tax office a nice chunk of your cash flow every three months. It's inevitable in the food business unless you're doing well enough to buy a large ticket item or lease, in which case you can claim that against the business and claim the GST.

Having an accounting software package such as Xero makes it easier to track all the spending that you do that does attract GST, such as cutlery, crockery, cleaning items, stationery, IT equipment, etc. As you claim back against these items, you are in effect saving the GST on the purchase, due to all of the GST you are collecting from your customers. Again, your accountant can advise you on this.

**Ensure you back up all your financial data and any business information, in case of fire or theft.**

### Tax debts

This advice will potentially save you a lot of sleepless nights. If you find you can't service your tax debt, especially in the early days, don't worry too much like we did. As long as you pay something towards it regularly, the tax office isn't that bad (in Australia at least!). They want you to succeed. You employ people, you pay your taxes (or will eventually), and you're part of the biggest employment sector in Australia. If you aren't paying these people, the government is!

I don't recommend this as a strategy but if you do hit hard times don't stress yourself, focus on making payments and catch up as soon as you can. We recommend putting a portion of your profit in another account purely for this debt.

### *Ben:*

*Just to set your mind at ease, I'd like to share with you that I had a sizable tax debt. How do you think I felt? I struggled for the first few years before I eventually got it down. I kept in touch with the Tax Office, let them know what was happening, and kept contributing something.*

Go to your taxation authority website for information about your reporting requirements.

**If you have a sizeable debt with the Australian Taxation Office, you pay interest. Make sure you keep in contact with them, ring them and make an agreement to pay off your debt. Sometimes this may take a while for you to pay it as you are continually accruing more debt (more GST and taxes). If this is the case, ask for a remission of interest where the interest you accrued may be removed from the debt. The Tax Office was very helpful for Ben, and he had thousands of dollars wiped off his debt. Imagine how that felt, the relief. Keep that in mind should you ever find yourself in a similar situation, however, please be clear we advise you do your best to avoid the situation to begin with.**

# CHAPTER 16

# SCAMS & RIP-OFFS

L ights attract insects! So when your business shines, have the bug swatter ready. Hopefully we've kept you out of a lot of potential trouble by taking you through some of the hazards and important legal requirements of running a business, but there are still scams and ripoff merchants out there that may trap you.

When you're successful, there are people who will see your business as a way to make them money. You need to be wise to these things, as do your staff.

**Ben:**
*I'd like to share a few of the experiences that have cost me over $35,000.*

*You may be approached by a company that offers you an unbelievable deal on business equipment, with your phone line tied in, so it seems as though you're getting the equipment for free. WOW! If it's too good to be true, then it probably is (I'm sure you've heard that before).*

*I was approached in this way about an equipment bundle that included a security monitoring system, a flat-screen monitor (which really didn't suit my business in the first place), one blackberry and another phone. I can't remember what the salesman said, but he sucked me into the tune of $30,000. I worked out my mistake when the equipment became cheaper or obsolete after just a couple of years.*

*However, the contract went for five years, costing me $15,000 more than it should have.*

*Some companies that try to sign you up for these deals go out of business every two years or so and re-open under a different name. They won't honour your agreement as technically it wasn't them, despite the fact that they have the same phone number and receptionist. Basically, you're left to wear the cost of a bad deal.*

*When it happened to me, I refused to pay what I owed to see who would come looking, and it turned out a large bank backed the lease agreement. I fought them legally, and the matter was settled out of court in my favour. Part of my settlement was that I can't name the bank, but you might like to Google equipment scams reported by the media.*

**Be wary of people or random phone calls trying to offer you a deal or set up meetings, and always get your lawyer to read any lengthy contracts.**

## Fire extinguishers

In Australia, your business will be required to have the appropriate fire extinguishers around your premises and have them checked every six months or after being used. There is a particular group who walk into businesses and tell you that you're legally obliged to have the extinguishers checked, rather than offering the service and asking if you would like to take it up. The unsuspecting business owner or employee will often just go along with it.

*Ben:*

*The fire extinguisher inspector came to my business, and the manager at the time fell right into the trap. I arrived moments later to find a receipt for a few hundred dollars for extinguisher testing. I rang the number on the card left by the 'tester' and spoke to the person who had just 'serviced' the extinguishers. I couldn't believe it when five minutes later a lady who could have been my grandmother, wearing tracksuit pants and with no professional markings, walked back in.*

*I questioned her about who said we had to have the extinguishers tested. She gave me her supervisor's number. I rang the 'supervisor', and he showed up minutes later, parking across the road in an old beat-up Ford Falcon. He was an overweight slob wearing what looked like an old fireman's shirt that he'd used for gardening. An argument ensued, and I warned him never to come into my business again. I walked out and took his number plate and then rang the appropriate authority. They told me they were trying to track them down, but admitted they were powerless to stop them.*

*When I spotted them going into another café, I followed the 'inspector' out to observe him at 'work'. He took a fire extinguisher to a nearby parked car, popped its boot to retrieve a stamp, and stamped the metal plate on the extinguisher without even looking at it at all while having a cigarette.*

*You work for every cent you earn, so when you have to get your extinguishers checked there are reputable companies that specialise in it. Use them, not rip-off merchants who not only take your money, but leave your business vulnerable by not performing the work they claim to be doing.*

*Ben:*
**'Beer line scam'**

*I had enquired about putting beer taps into my bar but decided against it. A week later, when I was not there, a guy turned up and said he was delivering cleaning fluids for the taps. My staff rang me and told me what was going on. I spoke to him and said there was a mistake, as we don't have taps. After he finished speaking to me, he cleverly hung up before I had a chance to speak to my staff. Of course he told my staff that I had said to pay him. I arrived a few hours later to find my staff member had done just that. I exclaimed, 'What! We don't even have beer taps!' My staff member felt stupid, but I realised my mistake as well. Obviously this was an inside job – how else could they have known I was putting in taps? Chalk this one up to experience.*

**Make sure your staff know which purchases they're allowed to authorise in your absence. Always make them aware of out of the ordinary deliveries and never to pay cash unless you approve it.**

# Service providers

It's not in the interest of your providers to deal with you dishonestly in any sense, and if they do you'd hope they wouldn't be in business for long. Having said that, dishonest providers do exist.

# Suppliers

Be on the lookout for old stock or damaged goods – boxes of tomatoes that are rotten underneath, rotten lettuce, out of date dry goods, and stock that's been replaced with items you didn't order. Whether they're innocent mistakes or intentions to deceive, always examine the goods you have had delivered to make sure the order is correct and in good condition. Good suppliers will replace poor quality or faulty goods or give you a credit, and will be very apologetic.

You'll more than likely be dealing with the middleman, not the original producer when it comes to fresh goods, so find out which day they're freshest and try to organise deliveries for that day.

# Tradespeople

When dealing with tradespeople you need to be clear about what you want and be sure you get a written quote. The number of times extras are added to a bill is astounding.

Also, ensure that GST is included. You should never accept a quote as a cash job, as the invoice will probably turn up with GST added. Here in Australia, we don't advertise food and coffee for one price and then add GST later, so neither should they. The only exception is if you're doing business in countries such as the United States, where it's standard practice that all taxes are added on later.

# Customer scams

Ninety-nine percent of your customers are genuine and honest; however, here are some of the things that the small percentage who are dishonest might get up to.

### 'Can I run a tab?'

Running up tabs and not paying can be an innocent mistake, but can also be deliberate theft. Always grab a credit card, and consider checking ID as well to stop stolen credit cards being used. This is more prevalent at night where alcohol is concerned, but depending on the nature of your business and what you charge it may happen during the day.

Tabs can become problematic when people don't pay them and then you have to chase them up.

### *Ben:*

*We let a few very good customers run up bar tabs. There was one customer in particular who we took an interest in both personally and as a business. We gave him some credit when he was low, and my staff out of their kindness kept an eye on his wellbeing. One of the staff, who had considered him a friend, had him to Christmas dinner with her family. Slowly the credit grew, and she suggested that he needed to keep a better check on it. His last words to the staff were, 'I'll fix it up next week'.*

*He's avoided the business ever since, insulted that staff member who was a friend and lost the respect of a group of people who cared about him. I have extended credit a number of times and been burnt more than half the time.*

*Bottom line – tabs are almost essential given the way we do so much on debit and credit card. Run tabs but don't extend credit!*

### 'Can I pay later?'

When a customer gets to know you a little, they may ask if they can pay for their order at a later time. Most people are honest and honour their promise. Sometimes people come back a week later, or even walk out and come back to pay. At some point you'll get one who will do it on purpose who you won't see for a week or two. Then when they think you've forgotten, they will try it again. Be upfront with reminding them that they didn't pay you last time. You will get a sense of who is just trying to take advantage.

**'I gave you a fifty.'**
Always place the money above the till while you work out the change. That way you can guarantee that when someone claims they gave you more than they did, you know exactly what they gave you. Make this best practice for all your staff.

**Charity boxes/tins and tips jars**
Make sure all charity boxes, tip jars and the like are tied down or tamper-proof.

*Ben:*
*We caught a guy on parole on our camera stealing $4.50 in tips plus the guide dog collection box. The charity box was bad enough, the tips although not a lot of money, it belonged to the staff. We had him on video that went straight to the police and at the end of the day he was sitting in a jail cell. It was a sad case but true.*

**Random pocketing**
Ashtrays, statues, cups, coffee tables, cushions – if it moves someone can steal it. Think about that when buying certain items for your business, and maybe refrain from purchasing overly expensive accessories.

Make sure staff secure their personal belongings. We've seen mobile phones, wallets, cash and cigarettes go missing. Ensure staff secure their items and store them safely on the premises.

*Ben:*
*'Mango Man'*
*'Mango Man' could fit into a few categories in this book. He was a thief, frustrating, an aggressive customer and just unpredictable. We named him Mango Man as we didn't know his name, but we once caught him in our kitchen eating a mango. He began with not paying for his coffees, and then progressed to stealing cappuccino cups and annoying staff with incessant ravings. He took a liking to one of my team and would always come in asking for her and got verbally aggressive when told she wasn't there. He would come in and tell jokes, leave flowers for no one in particular and then steal our toilet paper.*

*After confronting and banning him, he continued to show up, abuse the staff and quickly disappear again. We reported him to the police but were told we had to get onto them when he was around – an almost impossible task given the response time.*

# Staff
We have both loved most of our staff and have always given them the benefit of the doubt, but we have been stolen from and lied to by staff before. It's unfortunate that we have to mention this, but part of the reason we're writing

this book is to make you aware of the pitfalls and realities of running a business. Stealing is not just limited to cash.

The ways your staff can steal include:

### Cash straight into the pocket
One scenario is where someone will walk to the till and pretend to put in a transaction. Watch for change being left around as opposed to being recorded. A well-placed camera will help avoid this. Staff can easily track the money they put in the till without ringing it up and retrieve it later in the day.

### Taking stock
It's easy enough to grab any stock you own, from food and drinks to dry goods. Make staff allowances clear so if anything else is removed it constitutes stealing. This includes consuming your products without permission. If you have anything close to its use-by date, you may choose to let staff take it rather than throw it out, but be clear on what they're able to take.

### Claiming incorrect hours
Occasionally people are late, and that's fine, but being consistently late, leaving early or blatantly writing the wrong hours is stealing. Excessive breaks can also fall into this category.

### *Ben:*
*I had one trusted employee who had signed on 30 minutes early for over a year and was never questioned about the hours he recorded.*

*When I looked at the pays one day I made an enquiry and found he had been doing it for twelve months, which adds up in monetary loss. When I asked him about this, he said that after being required to start early one day twelve months earlier, he thought that was his new start time. I said, 'Well you've either been half-an-hour late for twelve months or you're putting down the wrong time.' It was blatantly obvious he was lying, but as a long-term employee I said I would give him the benefit of the doubt and only retrieve half of what he was overpaid, to be spread out over a number of pays. He turned up late for his very next shift, so I had to let him go.*

### Handing back excess change to friends
Handing back excess change to known friends or associates is a common practice. A good till system should show anomalies, but it is not foolproof, so cameras will help.

## Giving items away

Giving away items is stealing. You pay for product and time in order to make money so that you can pay your staff. Make clear the theory about business to your staff. Point out that if people aren't making more money for the business they can't get a pay rise. They certainly don't deserve one if they cost you money by giving away products.

## Skimming

Skimming includes outright stealing of cash a little bit at a time, but can also be done by ringing up a cheaper sale and retrieving the excess cash later.

## Refunding

This is where someone will input a cancellation or refund and then pocket the cash. Most tills have a refund button. Refunds shouldn't happen that often, so make sure you can track them and examine them on occasion. I have staff write a quick note as to why there was a refund.

You work hard for your money, and you put everything on the line, so don't let anyone take that away. Be vigilant, do stocktakes, install cameras and be as nice as you can. People don't like to rip off people they like.

In 99.9 per cent of occasions, our staff are and have been honest. It's because of this belief, and the fact that we have good managers and have put security precautions in place, that we can travel or just relax in other people's cafés without worrying about dishonesty.

The temptation to get something for nothing can create issues for your business.

**We have cameras installed around the place for our protection and the protection of staff. They are relatively inexpensive, and you can access them anywhere in the world from a smartphone.**

THE CAFE GUYS

# PART 4
# EMPIRE BUILDING –
# WORKING ON THE BUSINESS

# CHAPTER 17

# MARKETING

Your first customers may well be family, friends, workmates and colleagues. Hopefully, they'll also tell their friends about you. However you shouldn't rely on friends and family for all your marketing. Unless you're well-funded, you may need to give careful thought to what types of marketing gives the most return on investment. Whichever method you choose, it's all about repetition and consistency.

## Word-of-mouth

The best form of advertising is word-of-mouth, which now includes social media. There is nothing better for your business than providing something good, having someone recommend you and you backing it up.

### Ben:

*I serve a kick-ass hot chocolate and people would walk in and say, 'I've heard about your hot chocolate.' I have served the same style of hot chocolate for 16 years now I have adults coming in for a drink reminiscing how when they were kids they'd come for a hot chocolate. Talk about repeat business.*

## Website

A website, or at least a webpage that people can visit for information on where you are, opening times and what you do, is crucial for a new business. They can be relatively inexpensive, depending on the functionality you require. Your website can allow customers to browse your menu, make bookings, organise catering and make enquiries. You could even add a shopping cart functionality to sell promotional products and event tickets. Keep in mind this is another opportunity for your business to create an impression and is an extension of your business. Make sure the page is clearly laid out and easy to navigate and find information, while maintaining consistency with your brand, image and style.

# Google AdWords

Google AdWords is a program that allows you to position an ad for your website in Google's search results. Next time you Google something, look at the top few ads and you'll likely see the word 'Ad' written next to them. These results have been created through Google AdWords. The cost is a couple of cents each time someone clicks on your ad, and if you pay extra your site will potentially gain better exposure.

If your café is in Elwood, Victoria and you host events, you may add words such as coffee, Elwood, Melbourne, music, wine, venue, and so on. When someone types in any one or a combination of these words, it pushes you up the list of websites to view.

# Social media

Social media marketing is a profession in itself. At first you probably won't have time to keep on top of everything, but if you have a smartphone you can do a few things quickly and easily. Below is a list of some things you can do. Keep in mind social media is endlessly evolving, so it's worth finding someone who can help you out and if your budget permits, pay someone to do it for you. It can be quite time consuming, but it should be a priority for you to post regularly to make sure you remain in the forefront of your audience's mind. Aim to post at least once a week, and make sure your pictures are visually appealing and sharing examples of what you offer. This doesn't have to be just pictures of your food - think latte art, your store full of customers enjoying your business, or views from a window. Keep it interesting and enticing.

### Facebook
Facebook is great for connecting with your customers. Create a business page and group where you can easily post news, events and specials. You also can get some good feedback.

**Facebook changes its algorithms regularly which is reducing the impact of posts particularly for business pages. This forces businesses to pay for boosts to increase reach. It's worth learning how or paying a consultant to increase the impact of your posts.**

*Ben:*
*Be wary! We had someone who advertised an event on our page who claimed that drugs were being sold from our premises. It was sad because not only were they up for libel, we would have happily promoted another one of their events if we had been asked. Yes, its competition, but we're secure and confident enough in what we offer to happily suggest alternatives in our area.*

**Twitter**

Twitter is another good forum if you keep a regular dialogue going. Neither of us decided to use it because we didn't consistently tweet, but it's used successfully by many businesses.

**Instagram**

In the hospitality industry right now, Instagram is the go to social media platform. It captures a large audience and is useful for posting images and for quick engagement. You can grow your audience much faster than Facebook by using appropriate hashtags and engaging with influencers who run pages that are relevant to your business.

*Petar:*

*Social Media Influencers are your ally when it comes to growing your business and gaining exposure. There are individuals who have anywhere from the tens of thousands to the millions of followers, and can charge accordingly to advertise your business to their audience.*

*I used this very effectively. On Instagram, I found pages dedicated to sharing the best cafe's in Melbourne and these pages had anywhere from 20-50,000 followers. To be featured on these pages would put you right in front of your market - people actively involved and looking for places to visit and discover. In my experience most of these individuals are doing it as a hobby on the side and getting to visit cafes and restaurants at no expense, or working on building their profile to leverage financially down the track, or even to gain photography experience and grow their portfolio and credentials.*

*I would message these pages, and provide some information about us and present photos of what we do and serve. I invited them to come in, and for a complimentary breakfast for them and one other person most would accept and take professional photos on hi-tech equipment and share it on their page. This would result in potentially tens of thousands of people in my city becoming aware of us, tagging and sharing with their friends, and basically guaranteed a spike in visitors.*

*Eventually, because we were featured on the higher profile pages, smaller (but still effective!) pages with less than 10,000 followers would come in as regular customers and share their experience on their page as a way of building their profile, which would continue the growth and exposure for our business.*

*This is where your networking, communication and relationship building skills come to the fore. If you can build a genuine connection with these people when they come in and look after them well, they are more likely to come in unpaid and unprompted down the track and still promote you on their page or if you would like them to come in for another campaign they will happily oblige.*

*This strategy helped take our cafe to the next level of success - however, this is not guaranteed. If you don't have an attractive offering (enticing food/drinks/ambience), the people who run these pages won't be interested despite your free offerings or financial incentive. It has to be in their interests and maintain the consistency and not compromise the standard and quality of their own profile.*

It's almost impossible to keep abreast of all the technology out there, but apps such as Instagram, allow you to post simultaneously on Facebook, Twitter, Tumblr and Flickr, and are useful when putting a quick picture out there and maintaining activity on more than one profile at the same time.

## Other sites and apps
There are online services you can register with that advertise deals on your behalf for a percentage of the value sold.

For example, you may promote one dollar coffees, they may take up to 50 percent of that, and you cover the cost of the coffee. This can help get you high exposure as thousands of people follow these sites and use the apps. Of course, you limit the number of coffees per person and have a limit on how many you wish to sell. The strategy is that people buying cheap coffee may become regular customers after experiencing what you have to offer (and will hopefully buy something else to go with their coffee!). The same can be said for offering meals this way though the financial risks may be greater. As long as you have done your sums you will be fine.

Yelp and Zomato are word-of-mouth sites, where customers can rate your business. Barbait advertises drink specials and happy hours. There are many other websites and apps that can promote your business for free or that provide event listings. Whether you choose to be active or not you may be rated.

### Ben:
*I had an average rating on Zomato but on a closer look only a few people had rated it. On Google, I had a higher 4.5/5 rating from more people and most users consider it as a guide.*

More apps are popping up every week, so search your smart phone to see the other ways you can promote your business.

**Supplying wifi in your business is something to consider in our tech savvy world. You do need to have limitations for downloads but people almost expect it. People may favour a café that has wifi over one that doesn't. A lot of small business owners use cafés as meeting spaces or to do research so it is definitely worth thinking about who your target**

market are, and if this is something they will factor into their purchasing decisions.

# Newspapers and Magazines

In the IT age there is less reliance on newspapers, as they also post online, but it may be worth considering and there may be strategies that can work for your business. For example, you could post regular specials in a local newspaper where clients can bring in a clipping for a two-for-one deal or a discount. This allows you to track the effectiveness of your ad. You may be contacted by local papers offering a special one-off deal. A warning – don't be persuaded by the line that you're one of eight selected for a page and editorial.

They're just looking for your advertising dollar, so you need to work out whether the cost is justified and if it hits your target market.

Most local papers are happy to do a free editorial on new ventures starting up, especially if you're doing something different.

Offering a selection of popular daily newspapers for customers to read with their morning coffee is a good idea, magazines to a lesser extent, but this again will depend on your demographic.

***Ben:***

*I made good contacts with the local journalists, to the point where they would contact me for a story or about a local issue. I had classes, an art gallery, an independent theatre, sold 'I love Footscray' t-shirts and held special events, all of which were news worthy at one point or another.*

*If you have a story or something interesting, share it!*

*One day I noticed a bit of commotion on the street. A fellow who was parking next to the railway line had accelerated when he should have used the brake and went through the fence and over a small embankment next to the train tracks. He was fine but hugely embarrassed, with his white Toyota Camry hanging at a 45 degree angle over the edge and holding up city-bound trains.*

*Knowing he was okay and that there were no journalists around, I took a photo and gave a local journalist a call. I submitted the photo to them for free on the condition they mentioned that the incident took place right next to my business. Just another mention.*

*My business became well known and harnessed a passion for the Arts, offering something alternative and new to the area. It changed with the scene becoming more bar like and a venue that supported live music. Because of this I had a lot of advertising going out via flyers for bands, people Facebooking their gigs and inviting friends.*

*Any opportunity to get an article published that mentioned my café and reminded customers of my business was worthwhile. Repetition, repetition, repetition. That's why billboards are placed on roadsides along your commute to and from work. You have to see it ten times before it registers.*

*Many free magazines and papers have free listings for events or performances.*

# Letterbox drop

Letterbox drops can be cheap but time consuming if you do it yourself. There are people who will deliver flyers for a small fee, but there are two things to consider. A lot of people don't want 'junk mail', and an article in the paper may cost about the same and reach a larger number of people. Still, it doesn't hurt, even if you just cover areas walking distance from your business when you have the time for a stroll.

# Sponsorships and community groups

Joining or supporting clubs, schools and events can be effective. The cost of a free meal or coffee is worth paying to get your name in front of a crowd of people. Find organisations that are sympathetic to your business and that you're proud to support.

**Ben:**
*I joined the local traders association and became president for about two years. I was often sought for comment, met lots of other business people and council officials, and had many mentions in local media.*

**Petar:**
*The area we were operating in had a passionate football supporter base. I reached out to the local football team and sponsored the Captain of the team for a season. This was effective because the players would regularly visit as our vision was around health and wellbeing, which provided convenience for the athletes, who would also then tell their friends who were in footballing circles.*

*Eventually the exposure from the football club lead to elite athletes coming in regularly and some even making it their game day tradition. As an avid football fan myself, this was a huge thrill and one of my highlights!*

**Don't blow your budget on advertising if you have limited funds. A good advertising campaign can be achieved easily on a small budget purely by doing what you do well. Word of mouth may be all you need.**

# Beware false prophets

Google is your friend, but bad ratings on sites aren't. We have both been a target for malicious people and we also occasionally get negative feedback. This is a real problem on food-related apps and sites. Luckily we had been around long enough to have plenty of good ratings as well. As long as it's reasonable and constructive criticism, use bad feedback to your advantage and try to better your business.

### Ben:
*From a recent survey, I found that my customers wished I kept my website up to date. That's good feedback, but in the past I was too busy. Now everything is posted in advance and people can be confident they'll get the latest news. Always be nice and don't swear when responding to customer feedback. It seems like common sense, but I wear my heart on my sleeve and am quite defensive of my business. Luckily my business partner is more level headed, and will quickly remove anything inappropriate that I post. I did once get some traction, as well as massive exposure when taking local authorities to task about an absurd situation, but it could have easily backfired. When you're starting out tread carefully.*

# Branding

Do you recognise the big golden arches for any reason? Of course you do. Since childhood most of us have seen that sign and started drooling. But branding isn't just the domain of large companies. Small businesses make up 97% of businesses in Australia. The survival of your business will depend on your brand's visibility and memorability.

Brand consistency is vital in the creation of an effective brand. This doesn't just mean focusing on consistency visually, but it's also the language that you use to communicate to your community (e.g. website, brochures, promotions, emails, phone conversations and in person), how you behave and present yourself, how you speak to and treat your clients and how you leave them feeling.

We tend to start and focus with the visual brand because it is what creates your first impression and it is the first thing people will judge you on. It's been said that you have 7 seconds to make an impression. This is no longer the case. You will be lucky to get 3. A strong visual brand can help build trust, reduce buyer's resistance, and speed up buying decision. Consistency is important because the more people are exposed to your brand, the more they will trust and be open to buy.

Everything about branding ultimately leads to one important end result, and that is how you leave your customers and community feeling. Does your visual brand create a positive emotion when your customers come in contact with it? Does your product or service offering speak to their emotional needs? Is your customer's experience with your brand from first contact, to the purchase, through to the experience of using your product or service leave them feeling great about themselves? Achieving this will result in having a community of advocates who will gladly tell the world about you.

### Ben:

*I started branding my business a few years ago. We redesigned the Dancing Dog logo and printed T-shirts, beanies, key rings and even launched our own line of coffee. The Dancing Dog has been recognised across town, and my 'I love Footscray' T-shirts have been seen around the world and randomly spotted in countries such as Cambodia, Thailand, Scotland, China and the US. Our customers are taking our branded T-shirts with them on holidays and sharing photos of them with us through social media and emails. Branding builds communities and this is just one example of how branding connects people.*

### Petar:

*Branding really is everything. Your logo and all of your branding needs to suit the style of your business, and be consistent with your theme. Because our logo, branding and consistency was so fluid, on more than one occasion people asked whether we were a franchise. A couple of people were actually convinced we were a franchise and said they had seen another "Crimson Bear" on the other side of the city! This was impossible, as my business was the only one and most definitely not a franchise. It was however the ultimate compliment to our branding, marketing and communication.*

*I also created garments for staff to wear with our logo on it. Very simple long sleeve and short sleeve tops with just our red bear on the front. I made the logo (and the bear) very distinct, so it could be recognised anywhere, but also attractive on its own. We received a number of enquiries from customers regarding our clothing, that I made a small order to sell. We sold through that order very quickly, and I then made another bigger order and broadened the range. We sold out of all that stock as well, and merchandise then became become a standard part of our business.*

*Another factor in the success of our merchandise was my motivation when creating it. I wanted to be able to wear it to work, and then straight into the gym. It was essentially streetwear/activewear. As my market were predominantly active people, they were drawn to this and willing to purchase it.*

*There is no better feeling of accomplishment and appreciation than people loving what you do so much that they're willing to advertise your brand on your behalf. It's definitely a sign that you're doing things right.*

Creative professionals have the expertise to know how to work your brand to introduce new elements for higher attraction and engagement and still keep the consistency of your brand essence. Choosing the right creative professional can make or break your brand. Design can be taught but creativity and having an eye for what works is a skill that can't. Use a professional to guide and direct you as you go, but don't go overboard on budget.

# CHAPTER 18

# DIVERSIFYING

Something you may want to consider is what other services or items you can provide to your customers.

A lot of cafés, bars and restaurants do well with their core business and don't need to diversify; however, it could mean the survival of your business.

## Products

A lot of cafés sell produce they use in the business – coffee is the obvious one. Visit cafés and you'll often come across pre-packaged items available from a supplier, including tea and coffee, brewing equipment, teapots, strainers, jams… all sorts of things that put more money in your till.

We've sold merchandise and other products. You can sell anything and sometimes the quirkier the better. Just make sure they're quality items. There is nothing worse than seeing old bits of merchandise that are covered in dust being offered up for sale. When your place comes together you can see what may go with your theme.

In line with your marketing and if it suits your place, you can brand and sell reusable coffee cups, t-shirts, caps, and mugs. The list is only limited by your imagination. Replicate what franchises do, such as lines of biscuits and syrups.

*Ben:*
*At one point we were baking our own biscuits. We had a boutique coffee company supplying us who ran coffee carts at markets as well. We managed to subsidise our coffee costs by selling our cookies back to the coffee company. They eventually outgrew us but it was an extra source of income for about 18 months.*

*I also ran indoor markets with about 20 stall holders; garage sales to get rid of things I had accumulated, bulk art sales, and I had a staff member who ran a designer and vintage clothes market. I also had people run their flea markets on the premises for a commission of sales. All these generated extra coffee sales, brought new people into the venue and provided free advertising via editorials from local papers.*

# Catering for groups

If you have the ability to do bulk catering it's worth canvassing local businesses, clubs and groups. Catering can be great revenue when you get large requests. This is because it doesn't take much more effort to cater for 50 people than it does for 20. Put together sampling plates for local businesses and find out who books their catering.

You need to work out if you have the ability to deliver, you may need a car, and you may have to roster extra staff when you have a booking. All this can be well worth the effort.

# Room for rent

### Ben:

*I took on a two-storey building with the vision of filling the first floor with natural therapists while people relaxed in the café downstairs. I wasn't getting the therapists I needed to cover upstairs, so I focused on the café and looked at other ways to make the space work. I used one room as a gallery but also rented it out for functions and classes. My venue hosted several yoga classes, salsa, African drumming, belly dancing and a few other classes came and went. At one point, rental from these classes paid half the rent for the business.*

*Start your own club if you have the time and energy – that helps bring customers while supporting your local community. You can offer your venue for meetings if it's suitable, and this could boost numbers at quiet times and potentially some rent. If you have the space, co-working spaces are all the rage for people who don't need a full-time office.*

Be sure to leverage the most value out of your assets. Whether it be extra floor space or the extra coffee machine you ended up purchasing, you need to work out how that expensive asset is going to give you a better return. That probably means be prepared to think 'outside the box' in terms of what may bring more customers and energy to your café.

# Art

You may not have the space for classes but you may be able to decorate your place with art of some description and command a commission. Your walls are only holding up the roof, so why not make them work for you?

**Ben:**

*I ran a successful art gallery within my business for three years. I would charge 30 percent commission, plus the artists were required to have an opening party with a minimum spend. It was great on many levels. I'd get one good night; maybe some commission and most shows generated one or more articles in the local papers. My biggest commission was over $6,000!*

*I had an opening party for an artist who wanted to supply her own band, which was no problem from my point of view. Opening parties are about creating a buzz and loosening wallets and purses with a few glasses of champagne. Imagine my surprise when there were more people in the band than at the opening. She commented how it would have been nice if more people had shown up, and when I asked her about how many people she invited the answer was none. They had a great night, but other than my minimum fee it was a disappointment. Thank goodness there were a few sales throughout the exhibition. The lesson in this is to be very clear about what you expect from anyone hosting events on your premises. Make sure they understand their responsibility for getting people to the event. As much as I found it amusing I was learning that my time was valuable and so was my space.*

## Performance

Cafés make great spaces for intimate music, poetry or theatrical performances. You can work out a deal on the entrance fee if it's a ticketed event, or at a bare minimum you should get some extra people in the door.

**Ben:**

*I charged 30% of the entry fee for any event that was not run by me and run for profit, and if I was in doubt about how many people would come I'd charge a rental fee for the space.*

*The Dancing Dog hosted open mic nights for a number of years. An open mic allows anyone and everyone to get up and do a small performance, and musicians of all calibres come in and play for the love of music or even practice new work. It attracts everybody, both professionals and amateurs and is an excellent supportive environment if run well. It's important to have someone who is committed and passionate about running the night. We have also run a fortnightly poetry event for 13 years. It was initiated and is still run by impassioned poets. I supply a space for free and they promote, regularly use and fill the venue.*

*I also assisted in establishing the Dog Theatre within the premises, which ran for about three years. A great relationship which saw an independent theatre survive and win best venue in the Melbourne Fringe Festival. This required me to give up space and at times ticket sales were sparse. However, when a crowd attended a show the café received rental and had good alcohol sales, which was a great support to the business. While the café provided a home for the theatre, the theatre paid it back not only with extra income, but a great relationship with the director meant I was able to have some time away from the business while someone looked after it for me.*

There are many ways to diversify which are only limited by your imagination and if something doesn't work you can always try something else. Just be careful that whatever you do doesn't end up costing more than it's worth in income.

# CHAPTER 19

# TRAINING

Training is something that will become an ongoing part of your business and is just as important for you as it is for your staff.

We both started with minimal knowledge of the hospitality industry, and learnt everything from coffee-making skills, basic accounting, management, public relations, cooking, baking and cocktail/smoothie making along the way - just to name a few.

But before we look at different types of training, here's a cautionary tale.

***Ben:***
*Hanna was the first person I ever employed and started work on the very first day I opened. Towards the end of the day I asked Hanna to start the dishwasher. I was using domestic appliances as I couldn't afford a commercial dishwasher yet. I walked out the back for a minute and when I came back the dishwasher was on.*

*Five minutes later the bar was full of bubbles and suds. It was like an indoor music festival.*

*Hanna had put dishwashing liquid in the machine instead of dishwasher detergent. She had never used a dishwasher before as they didn't have one at home. Repairing the dishwasher cost me more than our first day's takings.*

An important lesson from day one: don't assume that your staff know everything! Go through everything staff need to do - no matter how seemingly basic. There can be many ways to perform certain tasks. Be specific as to how you would like it done in your business to avoid confusion and inconsistency. It is worth either writing a manual or keeping laminated cards for easy referral to maintain consistent communication and make it easy to train new staff.

# In-house training

Depending on the skills a new employee has, he or she may only need a basic training when they start, or you might just need to give them a working knowledge of how your place operates. You generally do this on the job and in the course of normal business.

Consider easing them into it. For their first few shifts, avoid rostering them during your busiest periods. This gives them an opportunity to learn how you expect to do things, and other staff to be able to give them attention and guidance where required. This also allows opportunity to build rapport and understanding.

Now if you're the novice like we were, you should employ people who know more than you and they can teach you. We have had several excellent staff from whom we learnt new skills or improved existing ones. Always ask about work practices at their previous jobs, and ask them to share if they think you could be doing something better. You don't have to take the advice, but the information they share could improve the efficiency and/or productivity of your business - especially if they've come from a popular and busy establishment.

# External training

There are a few different options. There are formal schools in Australia such as TAFEs or universities that have hospitality courses. These cater to people looking to gain entry into the industry and become chefs or other professionals. Finding courses is as simple as searching on the internet.

The other option is using Registered Training Organisations, whose business is to train people. There are government incentives to upskill people, so RTOs may offer to give you a subsidy on completion of the course, providing your employee meets certain pre-requisites. This could be worth thousands of dollars, depending on the trainee's age and any courses they have previously completed. Trainers will come at a time convenient for you, go through core subjects and tick off certain competencies.

**Ben:**
*I always taught staff coffee-making skills, so after demonstrating to the trainer that they could do this they were deemed competent. Technically this isn't free, and the RTO takes two payments. They attract funding for every student they pass, and they take a fee from your subsidy of between $700 and $1,400. Still, it's a win for everyone as long as the trainee completes the course.*

# Industry experts

This term can be used to describe anyone outside the business who you ask to teach skills to your staff. We both honed our coffee making skills by asking company reps to give some informal training to us and our staff.

It's in the company's interest that you produce the best result – you're representing their product and increasing their sales.

**Ben:**

*I also ask wine and beer reps to provide informal training, as well as any supplier that I think the staff could gain more experience or knowledge from. They also make great team-building events for your organisation.*

*I had a staff member who was prodding me to tell him what a great bartender he was. Constantly asking, 'Am I good? Am I good? I'm a good bartender aren't I?' Now he needed to work on a lot of skills and simply serving a customer isn't all there is to it. So my answer to his question would have been 'no', but I had to find a tactful way to show him that he still had a lot to learn. I asked a simple question, 'What wines do we stock?' To which he stared at me blank-faced and couldn't answer. To his credit, he learnt all the wines after that and was very enthusiastic when we had a little wine tasting with staff. He became a far better barman and continued to improve eventually taking his skill overseas.*

# Self-development

Bottom line – your business can only grow if you're prepared to grow, and training is not just for your staff, it's for you as well.

Have you heard this? You know what you know, and you know what you don't know, but you don't know what you don't know. Let me explain. You may know how to make coffee. You know that you have no idea how to do your bookkeeping, so you don't know that in Australia a $300 tax break is allowed for businesses with kitchens.

**Ben:**

*I only heard about this after eleven years in business. That equals one month's rent!*

The point is to keep searching for information on business and cafés and you'll keep finding facts, laws and ideas that you never knew existed. The best thing you can do is develop your faculties, read up, get to trade shows and network. It's as simple as talking to anyone and everyone. You'll be amazed at what you learn if you're open to learning and increasing your knowledge.

Do whatever courses you can find, and if you're time poor, which in the beginning is quite likely, look at distance learning or online courses.

Don't just study business materials, also study books that nourish your mind and soul that will help you be better and grow as a person. As you open your mind, more like-minded people and opportunities will be attracted towards you. And as you grow, so will your business.

### Ben:

*After two years in business, we had started cooking more than just muffins, so I decided to go to cooking school. I enrolled in a full-time course, bought the knives and outfit and for six months off I went in the morning while working in my business in the afternoons and weekends. I had a ball and thoroughly enjoyed the experience.*

### Petar:

*The hospitality industry is a very unique, challenging and exciting one. I was constantly learning and studying how to effectively market my business, build relationships, hire and manage staff, create the best possible culture, introduce new products and increase customer awareness. This lead me to want to work with others and support other business owners and individuals in the supply chain to make the industry even better and more successful. I undertook studies on a part-time (mainly online) basis to become a qualified professional coach and consultant. I loved helping and supporting others so much to achieve success and growth that I'm now doing it on a full-time basis. I never even knew this type of occupation existed until I did more research and learnt more. You don't know what you don't know - and what you do learn could change the trajectory of your life!*

**Visit *www.thecafeguys.com.au* for free industry updates and recommended reading that can bring value to your business.**

# Mentors

Networking isn't all about mingling at functions and fielding salesmen at trade shows. Anyone new to business can benefit from some mentoring, and using your networking contacts is the best way to find someone to help you on your journey as a business owner.

This will give you incredible insight, ideas and clarity. You may have to work around their schedules, but it's worth every second. Offer them lunch or a drink at your business so they can check it out. Don't be afraid to ask; people love to help and who doesn't like being asked for an opinion?

One key thing here is to listen and take the knowledge and advice on board. This is not about your parents telling you things as a teenager when you think you know it all. Your mentors' time is valuable, so don't waste it by letting good advice fall on deaf ears.

**Ben:**
*I had some mentoring when I began. I made the effort to see Steve wherever he was and at whatever time he was available. One day I told him that I really appreciated his time and asked why he was so ready to share everything. He just said it was because I listened, and I wanted to learn. I suppose I was a sponge for information as I realized I didn't know anything.*

**Petar:**
*I was constantly striving to improve, so was always engaged with mentors who I thought could teach me what it is I wanted to learn more about, and how to get there. If you want to reach a particular destination, the best way to get there is to ask someone who has already been. Reach out to people who have achieved and have the knowledge around what you want and follow their steps. It may require financial investment, but the information can save you ten or twenty times that in mistakes, or make you ten or twenty times that through your business and life's journey.*

**Local councils often run free workshops, offer access to mentors and hold networking functions for local businesses.**

# Listen

Listening is one of the most underrated skills of all. Learn to listen as opposed to hearing. Listen to everyone and everything, particularly staff and customers. If you listen more than you talk, you will find people warm to you and will give you all sorts of information.

Consider your everyday conversations. Do you formulate what you're going to say before someone finishes talking? Are you replying before someone finishes the question? Do you talk over people? Then you're not listening.

# Coaching

There are a variety of coaches who help you become more efficient and help steer you in times of need. If you have the money it is worth it, however two pieces of advice:

• Don't take too much on at once otherwise you won't get anything done.

• If you don't listen to the advice you pay for you may as well be throwing money away.

A coach can give you all the tools, advice and resources in the world, but if you can't commit to following it or don't have the right attitude towards it or an open mind about different ways to view your business, you won't get the desired results. It will be the equivalent of going to a Personal Trainer to get fitter and lose body fat but not wanting to exercise or take their nutritional advice and not getting the outcome you were looking for.

Don't take all advice for gospel, and like with any service based industry such as accountants and lawyers, ensure you find a coach who is credible and aligns to your own values and is compatible to you. Don't engage with someone who hasn't achieved the results you are looking for on some level.

### *Petar:*

*When I was working in my corporate career I began to feel unmotivated, lost and unfulfilled. I was lacking passion and knew I had more to offer, but didn't know how to harness it. When I began my journey into business, I had much to learn and understand. I was looking for some sort of consultant or mentor, but really struggled to find what I was looking for and even ridiculed because "I have a business degree, why would I need a business advisor?". It wasn't until recently I realised the coaching and mentoring industry existed, and I can now see not only how it would have accelerated my growth but also given me clarity, support and accountability I needed. The process of becoming a coach myself has now helped me map out what strategies I used and made me more aware so that I can articulate it and share it with others - i.e. People who were in a similar position as myself when I was looking advice, clarity, direction and success.*

# CHAPTER 20

# SELF-CARE

This may be stating the obvious, but look after yourself.

You must take time out. This seems obvious, but when you're deeply involved physically and mentally, and especially if you're feeling the financial pinch, you can quickly find yourself under pressure. It can start with not sleeping and not eating properly as you're endlessly busy and have little time for exercise and self-care.

Remind yourself why you started this business. It was for you, wasn't it? To make a better life for yourself.

So here are a few suggestions, most of which you have heard about, but we urge you to make them part of your schedule.

## Time management

In business many things need your attention all at once. You'll be working on accounts and then your power goes out, your coffee machine goes, a staff member calls in sick. It goes on and on. It's a real skill to change focus frequently without compromising the quality of what you're doing.

You will be under enough stress as it is, so learn how to manage your time if you don't already know. This means staying focused and learning to delegate. You can't do it all, so trusting staff to accomplish things is the only way you'll ever get to work on your business rather than just in it.

Priorities are important. Decide what you need to do, then focus on that task until you've either finished it or have gone as far as you can at that point in time. Re-prioritise and keep working through your list and you'll be far more efficient.

Here's a little hint. You need to remain operational so money flows. If a crucial aspect of the business goes wrong in some way, drop what you're doing and take action to correct it immediately. Once the repair is organised, you can resume what you were doing.

# Rest

Make sure you have quality time off with your partner and/or family, as well as time off for yourself. This is not time off where you run around and pay bills or play catch-up. Do your best to switch off and disconnect from business matters. Do the things you love - exercise, music, movies, video games, reading, catching up with friends.

Be clear with staff, managers, and any other contact for that matter that you are out of action and be specific with circumstances for which you would like them to contact you.

### Petar:

*I loved my business and wanted to know how things were going on any given day - even my "days off". I would request the manager check in with me through text message at certain periods during the day to give me a brief update on how we were going. They knew they could contact me if there were any challenges or emergencies but knew it was my day off and respected that boundary.*

# Massage

You'll probably develop sore muscles if you're on your feet all day. A full-body massage on a regular basis will help relax both your muscles and your mind. If you feel you can't afford it, go to a 20 minute massage booth in shopping centres. You can alternate with different parts of the body each week.

**Some of your customers are likely to be therapists in all sorts of fields. If you want to try to save a few dollars you could offer to barter and exchange services for the equivalent in food and coffee.**

# Meditation

If you don't have time to attend classes, it's as simple as grabbing some music or doing a guided meditation and clearing your mind. Is there something that you enjoy so much that you think of nothing else? Do it.

**Ben:**

*My self care activity is surfing. The moment I paddle out I am completely absorbed by the ocean and feel as though my mind is cleansed and I come back inspired. I would also often go for a walk in a park near the café for 15 minutes, just to clear my mind.*

# Talk

This is where broadening your network is important. Being able to regularly catch up with business owners who can relate to you and you can share issues and solutions with will help you manage yourself better. This way you won't have to take your business issues home and will allow you to be present with your loved ones.

**Ben:**

*I'm both thankful and apologetic to my girlfriends over this period. I would talk a lot about issues, and many times wouldn't be fully present as I was dwelling on something.*

**Petar:**

*Most of my friends and family members weren't entrepreneurs or business owners and I felt they couldn't relate to my journey or challenges, so conversations about my business with them were very "surface level". I didn't think they would understand - some of the simple conversations I would have with them gave me enough evidence of this - and didn't want to burden them either. If I was to do things differently, I would definitely put more work into engaging with others on a similar journey and making time to catch up with them. When I did connect with those people, the feeling of being understood was a weight off my shoulders. Whoever it might be for you, find people you can talk to and confide in.*

# Exercise and Nutrition

Any healthy lifestyle requires exercise and a balanced diet. Exercise may be the last thing you feel like doing some days but try to schedule a few sessions a week. Get into a routine, and as you may well know the fitter you are the more energy you will have. Do what you enjoy and being consistent with it will be easier.

Whether it's the gym, boxing classes, running or some other physical activity, make it a regular part of your lifestyle. Focus on what you're getting out of it and how you are bettering yourself each session. It will give you something to focus on and channel energy into outside of the business.

In addition and arguably more importantly, be consciously aware of your eating habits. Ensure your diet is based around consuming whole foods that will keep you healthy and in optimal condition to be the best you can in your business. Don't fall into the trap of processed fast food and convenience as developing this type of habit will be detrimental on a number of levels, including your energy levels, wellbeing and ultimately your business. It becomes all too easy and familiar to regularly choose unhealthy takeaway options and can be a difficult cycle to break once it becomes part of your routine. Create positive and resourceful habits and behaviours around this. Plan and prepare meals and snacks that are going to serve your purpose.

### Petar:

*In line with the vision and theme of my business, I loved going to the gym regularly and still do. The challenge of consistently improving my strength and endurance is my outlet, and I love that results manifest themselves both internally and externally. The regular exercise helps my mental clarity and kept my energy levels where I would need them to be for long days in the business serving customers. The days I didn't really feel like it - especially in the beginning - were challenging. Motivation wasn't always high, but those are the days that helped build my discipline around doing what I needed to do, not just when it was convenient for me (including getting up at 4am just to fit in a gym session). That approach has served me well across all areas of business and life.*

*I was the face of my business so I wanted to make sure I reflected what we were building, but I genuinely enjoy my time in the gym. Just me, my headphones and some heavy weights! Despite working in a health food establishment, I only ate there occasionally because I liked the habit and routine of my own preparation from home (which was similar to what we served anyway - but that isn't the point). This way I didn't spend time at work thinking about what I should have for lunch and preparing it there. The less trivial things I need to think about while in work mode gives me more time to focus energy and attention on more important tasks.*

## Stay positive

Smiling, laughing and enjoying the moment should be your approach. You should do this not only for yourself, but also for others. What would your impression be if you went for a morning coffee only to be greeted by someone who looks like they don't want to be there? If you are someone who finds it hard to smile and be happy and approachable, you better make some damn fine coffee to keep them coming in, as that's the only reason anyone would want to return. It's important to instill this knowledge in your staff too.

Customers don't come in to hear about yours or your staffs problems. They will come and continue to return for a positive experience.

### Ben:

*I'd start my day by pumping up the stereo, playing a song that I loved, singing and occasionally having a dance while I set up for the morning.*

# Write

Keep lists and a diary. It's ineffective to try and keep everything in your head and easy to forget it when you get distracted. If you keep notes you only have to remember one thing… where did I put my diary? This will keep your mind clear and focused on the task at hand. If something pops in your head, make a note.

Knowing you have made a note relieves a part of your brain that is quietly reminding you what needs to be done. This energy then can be used for being creative.

# Celebrate

Enjoy your achievements and triumphs, no matter how small. It's very easy to get caught up in the day to day and miss the little victories on your journey, however these little milestones will add up and you'll be able to look back at how far you've come - but don't wait to look back. Allow yourself to acknowledge all your wins along the way. Always pay more attention to what is going well and what you're grateful for rather than what's not going as well as you'd like. It's all about your vibe, and customers and staff will pick up on it and get involved in whatever is getting you excited.

# Learn to trust

No-one will ever care about your business as much as you do, and often they will not do as good a job as you. So if you find a person who comes close, love and cherish them and keep them as long as you can. One of the biggest mistakes an owner can make is to not trust staff. If you don't have confidence in them you can never relax.

**It really is worth your while to install security cameras in your business. They're inexpensive and not only will they protect your property and your staff; they will give you peace of mind in more ways than one.**

**To be realistic you will likely be a control freak to begin with as it's your baby you are leaving behind. With cameras you can have a quick look and see that the wheel still turns when you are away.**

*Ben:*
*In my first two years I barely took a day off, even while operating six days a week. On my day off I would catch up on paperwork, or do some maintenance or cleaning. For the first three years I spent every waking hour thinking about my business, and up to eight years on I'd still find myself obsessed with some issues with the café.*

*During my first year in business I chose to switch off in what was probably the worst possible way. I chose to drink until my mind turned off. This wasn't good, of course, as my body wasn't getting the rest it needed. Had I gone on I have no doubt I would have become gravely ill. I was tired, stressed and irritable, wasn't sleeping or eating properly, and, of course, those closest to me bore the brunt of it.*

*The reason I had started my business was to provide an opportunity for people to try different things, such as natural therapies and healing classes in a welcoming venue. Despite having delved into the fitness industry, massage and other healing modalities, I wasn't taking time out and looking after myself.*

# CHAPTER 21

# EXIT STRATEGIES

O ne of the most important reasons to have a successful business is so that you can sell it. Yes, you possibly haven't even started yet, but one day it will be time to say goodbye to the business you have cherished and nurtured. And hopefully when you decide to move on, you will be selling up, not closing down.

So let's briefly talk about exit strategies.

### Ben:

*I thought of selling multiple times for different reasons. Sometimes the journey got overwhelming, especially on my own, the pressure immense and at times exhaustion unbearable. I hope we save you some of this via the information in this book. I had a few offers that were ridiculously low and a few time wasters. If I had received the offer I wanted I would have taken it and it would have been an equally great buy. Instead, I held out and continued and am happy for hanging in there as taking on a business partner was a good move. Regardless the time will come when it's time to go. This time almost came recently where we had as good as sold, we got the price we wanted, and the buyers were very keen on the venue. Unfortunately, the landlord made it excessively hard for them and as a result the sale fell through. We suffered majorly as a result and almost lost the business.*

### Petar:

*Selling was never on my radar during my time in the business. I wanted to create a business I loved first, get it as successful as possible, then review from there. Maybe another location? Maybe a franchise? As I didn't prepare with a focused end and options in mind, I was unprepared for a sale and what was involved. I made the decision to sell for personal reasons and it was a decision I needed to execute on quickly as we were expecting a baby and the way I was working wasn't sustainable to support my growing family. There was no problem attracting interest as the business was running very well. The only issue was in the unfamiliarity of the process and understanding what was involved. I could have made the business a much more attractive prospect by understanding the sale process and keeping it in mind as an option from day one. Fortunately I engaged a very good business broker who was able to manage the process and execute the sale.*

# Your sale price

As a general rule, your business is worth three times your annual profit, plus the stock on hand, plus goodwill. In reality, your business is only worth what someone will pay for it. This may be more or less than the equation above.

As a sole trader or partnership in Australia, your wages count as profit. You will either pay income tax on them or pay tax on them at the end of the year when you do your books and profit and loss. This is important if you're deciding to sell. If you employ other people to run your business, it will look less profitable on the books.

If and when planning to sell, you could replace staff by working full time, and save those extra wages instantly. This means an immediate increase in profit.

Increasing profits and reducing costs is a strategy relevant to every exit option, whether you advertise for private sale, use a broker or sell to a partner.

# Exit options

Your exit options depend on the stage of your business.

### Private Sale

If you want to go with a private sale, you can advertise on the internet and in local, state-wide and even national newspapers. There are some business magazines where you can advertise, so browse through the magazine racks at the newsagents and see if they feel right for your business.

### Business brokers

There are good brokers around but unfortunately some have reputations like used car salesmen (no offence meant to either). If you go down this path, try and negotiate to pay all fees upon sale and be clear about advertising costs. However, many brokers require an up front fee to initiate the process and commence advertising. Find out where your business will be listed and ensure maximum exposure. As we have warned previously throughout this book, be thorough in your research and ensure you are comfortable with who you are engaging with.

**Ben:**
*I'll issue a warning. I listed my business with a broker, who quoted inflated figures and charged me advertising fees. I had a rubbish advertisement in a business magazine which I later found out to be the broker's magazine. The fees for advertising were up front and I lost about $2,500. I never heard from the broker, but when I called to see if there was any interest I had three enquiries the next day..*

## Partnerships
Exit strategies should be set out in your initial agreement and your partner should have first preference to buy you out. Valuation remains the same but split into the appropriate portion. Be flexible when it comes to a partner, as either one of you may not have the money to fully buy the other one out. You can come to some arrangement to pay the debt off, but this should also be put in writing.

## Close down
Hopefully this won't happen to you, but just say you've had enough or gone out of business, your lease hasn't been renewed or you can't sell for some reason. List all your equipment and advertise it on any online classifieds site, and anywhere else that is low cost. Take any reasonable offers, and be careful not to hold on to your goods for sentimental reasons.

If you have an ongoing lease, be prepared to seek legal advice. Hopefully someone will want to take it over. There are advantages in taking over a lease for people looking to start up - it's a very cost effective way for them to get into business - and you might be able to move on some of your equipment in the process.

## Fielding enquiries
If you choose to advertise or list with a broker, provided the market's right and your business is an attractive investment, you should start to get enquiries.

The key with any enquiries is not to share all of your information, especially financials until you have your prospective buyers sign a non-disclosure agreement. A good business broker will manage the enquiries and arrange inspections, as well as ensuring non-disclosure and confidentiality agreements are signed before prospective buyers receive any information. This gives peace of mind that anyone receiving information about your business won't share knowledge of the sale or any financials to the public, allowing you to run your business as normal without customers or staff being aware.

You'll get tyre kickers, as we called them earlier, who have the potential to waste your time with stupid questions and aren't interested or just doing general market research. As time goes on and people see you are viable you will get more serious enquiries.

Whether or not an enquiry leads to a sale, try to use these interactions as an opportunity to re-evaluate and objectively look at your business.

# CHAPTER 22

# BELIEF SYSTEMS

There is one more thing to say which is more important than anything else in this book.

**'Whether you think you can or think you can't, you are right.'** – *Henry Ford*

That statement holds the key to your success. You need to believe 100% that you will succeed.

Yes, you will make mistakes. These are a part of the journey. Through these mistakes you have to believe that you will succeed, so back yourself and know deep down that you do have the answers. As long as you focus on your goals and believe the answers will come, they will. Just keep moving forward.

Every book written about success and successful people is based on a vision and unwavering faith. About knowing they will succeed, despite where they are or were at on their journey.

It's sad that some people will want to see you fail, but as you're going out there, out of your comfort zone, you will make others question what they're doing with their lives. Other business people will understand what you're doing. Make an effort to create a network of supportive people and remember all the key points of this book

You're doing this for yourself, and to create a better life for yourself on some level. Stay true to this and stay loyal to yourself - not other people - as you're the one who will live and die by your decisions, not them. By living your life based on the opinions of others you essentially are a passenger in your own life. Take the wheel and enjoy the ride!

# CHAPTER 23

# THE FINAL WORD

There is more than one way to create a successful and profitable café business. Different methods, variables and possibilities. The advice in this book is quite general and broad, while also leveraging our own personal experience. It serves as an overview for those looking at getting into the industry, particularly without any experience. For more customised and tailored advice for your venture please go to www.thecafeguys.com.au and reach out! We would love to hear from you while supporting and championing you on your journey.

**Ben:**

*I returned to my old work because I could; my business was running well and I had enjoyed what I had done previously. My business would never run as well without me there but I chose to trust staff and give someone a manager's role so I could enjoy the variety. When I returned to my old job, someone I hadn't seen in six years took great delight in saying with a smile, 'So the café didn't work?' You should have seen his jaw drop when I told him it was still going and I had a manager running it for me. His moment of pure delight was smashed to pieces.*

*Probably the best compliment I ever got was from a friend who had played the devil's advocate for me. Years later we were having a beer and during a conversation he simply said, 'You're a can-do person; you just go out and do it'. If you're reading this and going for it, then you are too.*

*I was approached a few times by business students wanting to interview me. They quoted facts and figures and talked of business plans and other topics, but there was no mention through the course of our discussions of the ability to take that leap, face the fear, and just do it. Once you step off it's all about persistence and consistency. You can reel off as many facts and figures as you like, but until you step off that's all they remain. Leave the statistics to other people, but have supreme confidence that you will succeed and incorporate this as the core of your belief system.*

*Business is a great teacher – it will teach you about life and it will teach you about your character. It will expose your weaknesses, which you should work on, but it will also reveal strengths and unleash your creativity.*

*I wish you a great journey and good luck.*

### Petar:
*I never thought I'd be in the position I'm in now, having successfully created, ran and sold a business I had no experience in, and now running my second business guiding and mentoring others. I don't recognise who I was just a few years ago.*

*When I committed to opening a cafe, I told myself "This isn't about the money. I would rather work 12-15 hour days for myself in a fulfilling manner and on my own terms than 8-10 hours for someone else in a job I didn't believe in. As long as I had enough money to support my family and take a break from time to time, I didn't need anything else". I learnt an important lesson here, because by focusing on my vision, on my customers and on providing value, the money came as a result.*

*Managing myself and my mindset was key throughout my journey, especially when things got challenging - and you will encounter challenges. I don't think many people held out much hope of me being able to create a successful business, given the nature of the industry, my lack of experience and of course as Ben mentioned above - the statistics. But so what? My approach was that I was either going to achieve what I was aiming for, or at the very least get experience and learn skills that I wouldn't be able to learn anywhere else which would create a platform for a new path for myself. There was no such thing as failure, it wasn't a possible outcome. With this attitude, I had nothing to lose and everything to gain. The regret of not going for it was stronger than any risk.*

*It was the best decision I ever made and an achievement I am most proud of. If you think you've got it in you, don't let others hold you back. Don't hold yourself back.*

*You've got this.*

www.ingramcontent.com/pod-product-compliance
Lightning Source LLC
Chambersburg PA
CBHW031944190326
41519CB00007B/655